The Other Side

T.M. Miller

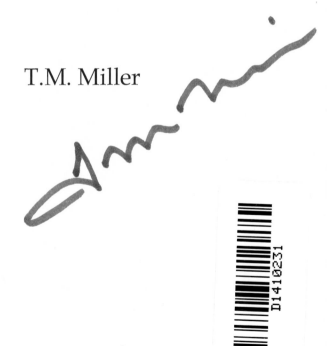

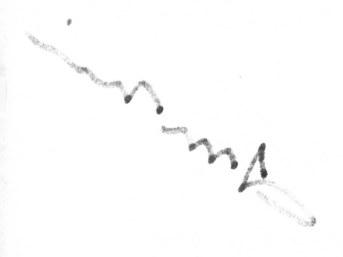

Acknowledgements:

Thank you to Curt Coleman, my father-in-law and the director of *The Other Side* documentary, for sharing your vision with me and allowing me to help you shape your story told here and in the movie. This has been a life changing experience.

Thank you to my wife, daughters, and mother-in-law, who put up with Curt's and my constant travels and supported me during times of emotional stress, when I time and again felt overwhelmed by the words of those who were so brave in telling their stories.

Thank you to my mother, who taught me to love writing and worked hard to make sure she maintained the integrity of my words while also ensuring that my work was well edited. I apologize again for being "wordy." You're the best.

Finally, thank you to all the subjects who told their stories with such grace and vulnerability. There would be no story to tell without your willingness to touch lives through our work. I hope I make you proud.

Table of Contents

Acknowledgements: 4

Preface 6

Section I: Stating Our Case.....................................8

Chapter One: "A Nation under Construction" 9

Chapter Two: "Enemy Language"..........................23

Section II: Backgrounds 37

Chapter Three: "Redeeming The Past"...................39

Chapter Four: "We Dream".....................................53

Chapter Five: "Falling In Love"...............................76

Section III: Horizons 89

Chapter Six: "Fostering Redemption"....................98

Chapter Seven: "New Communities" 106

Chapter Eight: "Pressing Forward to What Lies Ahead"....120

Conclusions: "I Want A Voice Too".......................145

Afterword: Thoughts From the Director 152

End Notes: 155

Preface

In 2013, soon after the election cycle was finished, Curt Coleman approached me to share a vision for a documentary. He wanted to challenge what was becoming the norm for public discourse. Discouraged with the level of animosity and contempt each side of the political debate showed for the other, Curt had come to see that people rarely looked past the talking points to see the real lives and people on the other side of any argument. Instead, people had begun to use various media outlets to vent hostility toward whole groups of people with whom they disagreed and often resorted to insulting *ad hominem* attacks upon strangers whose hearts, minds, and intentions the assailants could not know. As Curt has said many times since, we have accepted the premise that if we do not agree, we must be enemies.

Knowing from the beginning that to demonstrate our case we needed to share the stories of real, everyday people living in the midst of our culture wars, we talked for months about how to address the issue effectively. Through these discussions we developed an approach to make our case for civility, compassion, and mutual respect in the exchange of ideas and perspectives, an approach that would not put us in front of the camera to plead our case. We would have to find authentic subjects who genuinely agreed with our thesis. Our subjects, however, would have to share our vision while also telling their stories, which would represent one side of a controversial issue.

From the very beginning of the project, we believed that after filming was over, we would need a further step to elaborate and to ensure our purposes were not misconstrued. Curt asked me to supplement the film with a book through which we could go into more depth with each subject's story and also share our own thoughts about how to move forward as a nation.

In the first section, we present our argument in which we insist that prejudice and hatred cannot be dismissed as the problems of others. All of us have to take a stand against both, first in our own lives and then in our society, while we learn to share with those who are different from us.

In our second and third sections, we dive deeper into the stories of our subjects and expound upon their lives beyond that which the time constraints of a movie allow. In section two, we learn about our subjects' backgrounds, and, in section three, we see how their lives have made them people who stand for a cause but decline to see people on the other side as their enemies.

In our conclusion, we resume our proposition for a better way forward and call upon each person who reads and views our work to demand of our leaders nothing less than civility and respect in the public square. Our leaders are going to give us what they think we want. If we respond positively to hate and slander, we will remain in this futile cycle forever. What if a bipartisan community insisting upon thoughtful behavior from our leaders should arise? If everyday citizens are ever going to conquer our current malaise, we must use the tools at our disposal, and the best tool we have is a collective voice.

Section I: Stating Our Case

Since the beginning of our project, we have sincerely believed that the average citizen truly cares about the path and health of our nation; however, it seems that most average citizens do not really believe we as a people have much control over the direction of our nation. We do not want to see people embarrassed, hurt, or marginalized, but we do have major differences in opinion about what is best for our nation and our society.

We must get beyond this idea that we have no say. We must also get beyond the idea that someone else is responsible for the problems we face. If we are going to see healing in our nation, many everyday citizens must agree to do something about the intractable issues that divide us together.

The greatest impediment to the progress and equity we all desire is our long list of disagreements and our inability to afford others their opinions without dividing them into friendly and enemy camps. If we cannot set aside our partisanship long enough to seek areas of consensus, what hope do we have of ending the hostile tug-of-war in which our government and society are stuck? We don't deny the inevitability of disagreement, nor do we believe differences of opinion hurt us the most. Rather, we believe the real culprit is *how* we disagree.

Perhaps it sounds idealistic to say conversation is the key, and in some ways the description fits. Simply being civil will not heal all our wounds. It is, however, a start. We won't know how successful our premise can be until we try it, but we do know that the status quo isn't working at all.

Chapter One: "A Nation under Construction"

Facing reality

Inflaming the national debate over immigration, a shocking murder case has become the center of argument during this election cycle. After he was deported five times for illegally entering the United States, Juan Francisco Lopez-Sanchez was arrested in the sanctuary city of San Francisco, California for the murder of Kathryn Steinl, who was shot in the back while she walked with her father on Pier 14. Her last words were, "Help me, Dad." Lopez-Sanchez admitted to firing the weapon but claims his action was accidental. This case is still ongoing, and the suspect will face trial.[i]

In his groundbreaking book titled *The Working Poor*, David K. Shipler writes of a small work camp in a remote, rural area of North Carolina. According to Shipler, immigrants are shipped from Mexico by coyote smugglers, who charge well over $1000 to bring undocumented workers who do not have access to the amount of money charged. The people who run the camps agree to pay the fee and withhold portions of the workers' wages until their debt is paid. Held like prisoners, these immigrants are stowed some fifteen at a time in twelve by fifteen foot cinder block rooms near the fields where they work, the only amenity being a bare light bulb hanging from the ceiling. With no air-conditioning or beds, these men and women are essentially held captive in what can only be considered modern day slavery.[ii]

In March of 2016, an Atlanta, Georgia man was arrested for allegedly pouring a pot of boiling water on his girlfriend's son and partner while they rested in bed together. It is alleged that Martin Blackwell perpetrated this vicious attack for no other reason than the victims' sexual orientation. Blackwell has been charged with two counts of aggravated battery and will stand trial.[iii]

In July of 2013, two pastors attended a gay pride event in protest. A group confronted the two men and violence ensued. While a group surrounded the pastors, two men knocked the preachers to the ground and repeatedly kicked the pastors in the ribs before police broke up the altercation. Both assailants face misdemeanor charges.[iv]

In June of 2015, Dylan Roof walked into Emmanuel AME Church and sat through a prayer service. He then opened fire and killed nine black worshipers and wounding one other. Roof, admitting to the crime, claimed he was trying to incite a race war.[v]

From July to November of 2009, dozens from black street gangs in Denver, Colorado were arrested after they targeted whites as part of an initiation process. The gangs allegedly sent groups, sometimes in bands of twenty or more members, out to attack unsuspecting whites. The groups continually beat the victim after the person had been blindly attacked with a punch to the head. Reports of fractured skulls and broken ribs were submitted. During the attacks, racial slurs were hurled in an attempt to scare whites from certain areas of Denver.[vi]

These stories are examples of a much larger problem we face today. While we will focus on the issues of race, immigration, and marriage, these are simply a few of the divisive topics polarizing people into enemy camps. Many other issues divide our communities and cause unrest, but we hope that these may serve as case studies to highlight the manner in which affiliations that create an "us versus them" mentality cause unwarranted assumptions and harm toward others, as well as deep divisions in our communities.

As the examples above illustrate, hate is undoubtedly alive and well in America and across the globe. This book, as well as the documentary of the same name, is not designed to deny that this nation, as well as nations across the globe, harbors prejudice; rather, it will demonstrate that no group is completely innocent. Moreover, no single group can or should be understood as a whole based on the actions of certain members within that group. Within each group, advocates have denounced violent actions committed by their own members. Most people, no matter their group affiliations, do not want to be defined by the worst segments of their communities.

Examining our prejudices isn't pleasant work, but it is necessary if we are to redeem our society and elevate it to a point of greater civility. We must confront the sad and violent realties around us and find a way to unify against them. Otherwise, we will continue to mourn hate crimes and see the violence escalate. In turn, we may permit mayhem committed by members of other groups to fuel our latent distaste for the entire group and indirectly perpetuate the misunderstanding and prejudice at the root of our troubles. If we want to make even a modest dent in the unrest that divides us, we cannot permit divisive issues to grow unaddressed within our own communities. We must seek solutions.

Obviously, the current nature of public discourse, with the constant name-calling and finger pointing, is not working. We have become reactionaries. Instead of assuming at least some of the responsibility for the state of affairs and agreeing to have meaningful conversations in which opposing ideas may arise, our default response to each crime becomes an "I told you so" opportunity to prove our point. Talking about our brokenness only after something tragic happens and then resorting to arguments about who is really in the wrong solves nothing. We must start a conversation that begins with civil respect to discover how we can grow together before we jump into the fray yet again. Otherwise, the divide will grow.

According to *Time* journalist Eric Baker, people rarely respond positively to heated debates. When such arguments begin, one's ability to persuade another ends. Baker cites studies showing that once people realize their views are being challenged, their brains' capacities for logic and reason diminish while their fight or flight responses heighten. Though it is possible to persuade people, heated debate is not effective.[vii]

This book is meant for those who do not wish to act out in violence but often see no way forward. There are good people in every group, of course, and it is time we give each other our ear to hear how we might find mutual respect for the betterment of our communities.

Fighting prejudice

If someone had asked me to speak about prejudice when I began working on the project that would lead to this book, my response would have been rather dismissive since I was, to some degree, still in denial about the very real existence of the biases this project has uncovered for me. It is a strange thing to say, since a large purpose of this project has been to combat prejudice, but I have come to realize that we cannot combat prejudice on its terms. Prejudice refuses to listen and often attacks; therefore, even my response to prejudice must be more than an indignant reaction.

I would be remiss if I did not mention that I am no expert in behavioral sciences. Instead, I am simply a man on an investigative journey. After researching the topic for some time, I discovered to my frustration that experts offer very complex and even divergent opinions about how we should seek to resolve prejudice, if it can be resolved at all. With this in mind, when I speak of prejudice, I am using the term as it is commonly applied in everyday conversation and not in any of the nuanced ways that complicate the issue. I am not, however, limiting prejudice to the topic of race. For our purposes, prejudice is any unjustifiably negative view of a whole category of people that ignores the variations of individuals within all classifications of people groups. This is an issue that certainly can be addressed. Moreover, we do not have to be behaviorists to find solutions, but we do have to be thoughtful.

Lacking expertise has never kept me from studying issues of ethics and morality and dialoguing with others about what I have learned. Had I publicly addressed prejudice before beginning this work, I likely would have insisted that all prejudice comes from some malicious place in the human heart and advised all sensible people to avoid others who display any form of it. This naïve reaction would have been wholly unhelpful and perhaps dishonest, as I would have, through posturing, been trying to distance myself from any guilt.

Reflecting honestly upon my own encounters with prejudice, I must admit that my most effective breakthroughs in overcoming hate have come only when I have faced hate within myself. Without dismissing its malignant nature, I do not think prejudice is always a result of choosing to be hateful. Sometimes, it is a product of ignorance, which is not an excuse, but is a cause.

When our project was coming to a close, I sat down with Vernon and Portia Jackson, our subjects who discuss how to move forward with race relations in the midst of conflict, and we talked about how this process has impacted us all. I am a white male in my early thirties, and the Jacksons are a black couple in their fifties. We agreed that through the process, we grew together. We were open and vulnerable about our ideas regarding race; however, we also agreed that under normal circumstances, we would probably never have found the sort of friendship with each other we forged.

If we had met under typical circumstances, perhaps at church or a local ballgame, and if we had gone a step further to become friends, we still would never have spoken frankly and openly about race together. We would not have afforded each other the chance to see the world through a different perspective because it is not polite or comfortable to discuss such things.

While speaking to countless people about their views of others, whether "other" designates race, religion, political affiliation, or sexual orientation, I have found that good people on either side of the various issues are not above prejudging whole categories of people. In so many cases, it is not that these people want to be hateful. In fact, many of them are wonderful and kind and generous in many ways. Their prejudgments, just like those I have discovered in my own life, exist because they have never really gotten to know the other side but have spent years harboring unfavorable ideas and accepting unflattering caricatures from afar.

If I were to take my own advice to avoid all persons who ever display any measure of prejudice, I would have to walk away from society as a whole and then devise a way to avoid myself while I was at it, and I suspect you would too. There has to be a better way. We have to start a conversation. Arguments do not work, because their goal is not to hear, but to be heard. In a conversation we can do both.

Walking away from each other, even when the other displays prejudice, is not the answer. Certainly we should not wish to associate with persons who express violent hatred of others, but such people are not the real issue. We are not walking away from that segment of society that engages in violence towards others alone. In today's climate of polarization, we are walking away from anyone who shows any measure of disagreement with how we think the world should be because we believe the lie that we have nothing in common. Yes, it might be true that there are whole groups of people who think very differently than we do, whatever our affiliations might be, but that does not mean we do not share at least one thing in common: the intrinsic dignity that comes with simply being human.

What we must come to realize is that people do not deserve our respect and compassion based on the virtue of being right. As our Founding Fathers stated at the inception of this nation, a subject we will return to momentarily, people merit certain rights solely because they are people. They believed humans have the inalienable rights of life, liberty, and the pursuit of happiness. I believe it is reasonable to assert that we all deserve kindness and compassion from one another because as social beings, we affect each other's lives, liberty and opportunity to find contentment.

Fear has two natural responses: Fight or flight, the latter option being preferable. Sometimes ignorance exists, not because a person refuses to learn, but because he or she has never had the opportunity to see the world any differently. What if, by avoiding all persons who ever display overt gestures of prejudice, we who believe we are innocent deny these people the chance to see outside their own small vantage points? What if, by finally speaking to this other, we find that as we listen, we too are challenged by this person's unique point of view, and we, too, mature? In my own life, a lovingly firm challenge has on more than one occasion changed me for the better. I am glad that those who challenged me did not simply walk away. Understanding prejudice in this way, we can see that we all have ownership in how we come to understand each other.

Those who, like me, have deep convictions need not be concerned that this project seeks to undermine or vilify one side to benefit the other or challenge sincere beliefs. Rather, we would suggest that we can maintain a firm position about which we feel strongly yet find common ground and extend grace to those on the other side if we are willing to have a conversation. The nature of this project is to listen to people from various walks of life. Naturally, anyone who already has an opinion on any of the subjects we discuss will find views with which he or she disagrees since we present both sides. Our purpose is not to argue about who is right or wrong but to demonstrate that real people just like us who view life through a different lens have stories worth hearing.

Some have asked, "Don't you think that by giving people you disagree with a platform to share their views you are in some way supporting them or condoning their views?" On one level, this is true. By listening to them, I am supporting all of those who speak in this book on the merit of everyone's right to be heard, whether or not I agree.

Some suggest that merely listening to others is dangerous. Are we really worried about morality if we choose to ignore others? Morality cannot be simply about being right or having the right thoughts. It must also be about right living and behavior towards one another. The Golden Rule espoused by many belief systems seems to lose its appeal when it means we have to listen to others. Our nation's current polarization should be an indictment of our failure to do so. We have tried endless debate and found it wanting.

Disagreeing with someone doesn't mean we have to dislike or even hate each other, but believing so does make it easier to dismiss our ideological adversaries. In coming to believe that we have no common ground whatsoever, we open the door for prejudice to creep in and convince ourselves that the other wants nothing more than to destroy our whole way of life. Do such people exist on both sides of our various issues? I suppose there are, but can we categorize whole groups of people based on the extremists in their camps? Do we want to be affiliated with the fringe elements in ours?

Maintaining a polite distance from these issues won't work either because avoiding the issues that divide us reinforces the lack of understanding that nurtures unwarranted fears rooted in ignorance. Again, we have to talk and, more importantly, listen to each other.

Assumptions of Prejudice

Practically speaking, humans are biologically hardwired to make all sorts of assumptions, and these assumptions more often than not prove extremely useful in helping us navigate day-to-day activities. Assumptions help us anticipate. We anticipate what the traffic will be like at certain times of the day so that we can make the right decisions about when to leave home to get to work on time. We anticipate how much milk our household will consume so that we do not buy too much, only to have it spoil before it is consumed. We anticipate the likelihood of certain illnesses and ensure our children receive the vaccinations needed to prevent such. Assumption is practical, and it is the innocent cousin of prejudice.

Just as we anticipate how we will act in light of a million conceivable possibilities in everyday life, we anticipate how we are going to interact with each other in relationships, and we base our assumptions upon what we imagine the other will be like, whether we have known the person for years or are meeting for the first time. How many conversations have you practiced in the shower or in the car when no one is there?

In his book *Empathy*, Dr. Roman Krznaric explains this tendency:

> *The vast majority of us have assumptions and prejudices about others. We are prone to stereotyping, making snap judgments based on first impressions, and casually project our biases and preconceptions onto people while knowing very little about the reality of their lives...Some popular psychology books, such as Malcolm Gladwell's Blink: The Power of Thinking Without Thinking, argue that we are actually very skilled at making quick judgments about others — such as whether we are compatible with someone we met for just two minutes while speed dating — and ought to more readily trust our instincts. But our instincts can easily be infected by assumptions inherited from society and culture that have penetrated deep into our psyches. Gladwell admits that "our unconscious attitudes may be utterly incompatible with our stated conscious values..."*[viii]

One harmless general assumption is that business professionals are serious and demanding. Someone entering an interview with an unknown potential employer will likely consider it prudent to act in accordance with this general assumption to create a favorable impression. As a result, a whole market producing books, seminars, and personal coaches who teach persons how to interact with these professionals has arisen. Is it fair that society has so prejudged and stereotyped business executives for personal gain? They are people too. But, I want the job, and if making assumptions about the nature of the interviewer will give me an edge over my competition, then so be it.

Whether we like it or not, we often form our assumptions on a myriad of indicators, such as a person's race, religion, and social standing. Perhaps the worst thing we can do is pretend we are somehow above our natural human tendency to make assumptions. What we can do, however, is to test my assumptions by getting to know others and giving them a chance. The danger is not in making assumptions *per se*. It is making incorrect and unfair assumptions. We may never get it just right, but when we are content to assume our way of thinking and acting is the only proper way to think and act, our prejudice becomes the seed of something much more dangerous and sinister.

While human beings tend to make assumptions that lead to fear of "the other," and its attendant negative consequences, we are also capable of self-reflection, acknowledgment of our dispositions, and exerting a measure of control over what we tend to feel and assume. We don't have to be simply instinctual; we can also be intelligent. Therefore, we have a responsibility to check our fears often. Overcoming prejudice must become an intentional daily activity.

The Other Side project upon which this book is based is an exercise in helping others see beyond themselves to reveal that our assumptions are often misplaced, yet while working towards this humble goal, I have found I was not above making false assumptions. In fact, during one of our interviews, I ran headlong into a learning opportunity in confronting my assumptions (perhaps even a prejudice) once again.

Breaking the Mold

Over the course of the following chapters, we will

introduce several subjects who represent the human lives lived on either side of the culture wars dividing America. For now, however, we will discuss a particular event that arose in our discussions with Vernon, who, along with his wife Portia, was our subject for discussing racism in America from a black perspective.

Because of recent events pertaining to black Americans and their value in our society, it is fairly obvious that one of the oldest culture wars, the one that still burns the brightest today, is that which involves race. When we began searching for a compelling story from the black community, we found the Jacksons.

During one of our interviews, we asked Vernon to share his thoughts about our nation in general. We expected him to address current affairs, especially the strife we constantly see in the news concerning the state of race relations in America. As we suspected, Vernon did have much to say upon this topic, but he also took this opportunity to veer toward an unexpected road, at least for me, that explored his understanding of the "Great American Project" envisioned and created by the Founding Fathers.

The discussion of our history inevitably led to discourse about various injustices inflicted upon the Native American nations from whom the land we call the United States was taken and the African slaves upon whose backs much of the economic viability of our early nation was established.

It did not take long for me to make an assumption about where Vernon was going with these topics: As a black man, Vernon, I assumed, construed America to be built on the injustice that has fostered our intractable struggle with racism. I further assumed he was going to make a call to deconstruct and rebuild, a complete revolution, perhaps. Any discussion of the Founding Fathers would serve as a preamble to the discussion of continuing systemic inequality in the present. I expected him to insist that if that is where we started, that is where we would stay unless we changed completely. While

Vernon talked, I felt quite a bit of grief about our nation and our past.

To my surprise, Vernon, without dismissing the undeniable wrongdoing involved in our nation's beginnings, veered toward an unexpected path again when he spoke genuinely and fondly of the Founding Fathers "genius" and their thoughts concerning the self-evident and inalienable truth of the equality of all men, along with the rights that should be afforded to "everyone" based upon the rights of life, liberty, and pursuit of happiness. When he referred to these foundational ideas, despite his lack of bitterness, I was still expecting him to enumerate the obvious hypocrisies of those who penned these words, since they never treated Vernon's ancestors by the standards they espoused.

Instead, Vernon continued to speak highly of these founding principles: "I believe in this country. I believe in America. America was born on the concept of new life, new freedoms, new possibilities." For Vernon, what the Founding Fathers created was not a nation that had fully realized these truths, but a nation with the potential for such idealistic assertions to become actual truths lived out in the lives of every member of our society if only we would continually work towards understanding these truths. In Vernon's mind, we can still build a future that fully realizes these truths because of the foundation the founders laid.

I will never forget that lesson. Here I sat, wanting to contribute something to our nation through these interviews, a call for compassion in the public square at least, but really overwhelmed by the feeling that this probably was not possible, especially when Vernon mentioned a beginning that left so many feeling displaced and despondent. Vernon, a man who knows all too well the systemic issues that linger from such a past, displayed more hope than I had and challenged me to think anew. He made hope real to me.

Perhaps, as Vernon suggested, our Founding Fathers had conceived of an idea so wonderful that they, in their limited lifetime, could never fully realize. Vernon also pointed out that from America's beginning, all civil victories establishing the dignity of our fellow humans have been based upon the foundation laid by these visionaries. Perhaps, like Vernon, we are not to excuse any injustice; however, we might still understand this history as simply a starting point and a sign of hope rather than a failure to launch.

As a nation may we join all those visionaries like our Founding Fathers and see reformers such as Dr. Martin Luther King, Jr. and Susan B. Anthony, for example, as persons who continued to build upon a legacy, never assuming the status quo was good enough, but always believing in and hoping for newer horizons of possibility that did not end with them.

The possibilities for greater fulfillment of the founders' vision should motivate us to venture forward into the future together, even as we stand on the shoulders of those who came before us so that we may see even further. While there are many sins of the past we must acknowledge and address, the opportunity to build upon the proposition of equality for all is a heritage of which we can all be proud, a place where we can bring redemption to the past, peace to the present, and hope to the future.

Perhaps our nation's founders never knew the full possibilities of their own ideals. Perhaps they, along with many who followed, limited those possibilities, but we do not have to give up because one generation was not long enough to realize the full potential of liberty and justice for all. It is our duty to our still very young nation never to stop acting upon the possibilities of what it means for all human beings to have the right to life, liberty, and the pursuit of happiness.

Perspective

One of the last times I sat with Vernon in his home for an interview, a neighbor started his leaf blower. We were not recording Vernon only for the sake of this book but in hopes of a film as well, and we could not move forward with our interview until the noise subsided. Vernon stepped outside to see if his neighbor could finish his yard work at a later time.

When he stepped back in he said, "Well, I could have asked him to stop, and he would be more than willing. He is a very good neighbor, but I think he is almost done." Vernon paused for a moment, seeming to think of something else, and then continued, "He loves taking care of his yard, and I really like his American flag out front. It looks much better than mine. I have thought about getting a new pole like his. My flag is on a rough wooden stick, but it has meaning for me like that." Smiling, Vernon added, "America under construction."

Vernon sees our nation not as a nation that failed because we did not get it right on the first try, but as a nation with a heritage that is still becoming. That is a heritage of which Vernon can be proud, and his pride has engendered hope in my heart. It is time for America to reclaim this heritage. May it never be said of this generation, "Here is where America finally quit believing in its great experiment of procuring the rights of life, liberty and pursuit of happiness for all."

We all may experience some guilt in our current situation, but that does not mean we are all bad people. It might be difficult to have the sorts of vulnerable discussions it will take to move forward, but isn't our nation worth it?

Chapter Two: "Enemy Language"

Anger is a hell of a thing. Sometimes it is warranted, but most often, it is simply a reaction. When we are tired of working our way down the long path of doing things the right way or the opposition too often gets in the way and we just don't have the patience any longer to work things out, we explode. Anger, which often leads to irrational thoughts and actions, is efficient in one way: It helps us to solidify both mentally and emotionally, who our enemy is. It transforms complex matters into black and white issues for which there are no black and white solutions. Anger makes me right and you wrong, period. It creates an ultimate enemy upon which to shift all our problems. We have done this in many ways on a national scale. Should we let a single emotion dictate how we handle division?

Making Enemies

We live in a divided society, but one thing is for sure. In small town America, little else unites a community for a common cause like high school athletics. For several hours the whole town shows up—people of various means, color, and affiliations—and for a brief moment, we all cheer together.

Like many other high school boys in the South, I was expected to participate in sports as a means of character building. I chose football. I was not spectacular, but it was great to be a part of something so exciting and so unifying in my own community. Even with the other side a mere width of the field away, the people in the bleachers surrounding me were all for each other, and they were all rooting for the same goal: a win

On the other hand, there is nothing like athletic

competition to help a community find a common enemy. Not so witty banners denigrating opponents typically line the stadium fence or gymnasium wall. Most of the time it is all in good fun, although there are times things can sour. The cheers and taunts can become heated when the competition ensues.

The confrontation and occasional violence that can occur between opposing fans has always made me uneasy. I find it telling and odd that something as innocent as a sporting event can heighten our most basic instinct to attack others. If we cannot get along in places like the high school arena, what hope do we have for more serious scenarios? I think this is why a story my mother likes to tell about her former classmate's father stands out in my mind as an endearing example of hope.

Mr. Flynn went to see his son's first junior varsity basketball game, and when his son's team made its initial basket, he cheered loudly in support. Nothing special there. However, on the very next play, an athlete for the opposing team answered with a basket for the other side. Mr. Flynn again jumped to his feet with the same enthusiasm and cheered. When my mother, a young teen at the time, looked at him in confusion, he shrugged and said, "Hey, I'm for everybody!"

High school sports are just games played by young people with no group's being more worthy than the other, unless, of course, one is watching a Disney movie. Each child approaches the field, court, or mat to do his or her best, and, at least for this man from my mother's childhood, each deserves our admiration for that, even if some of them are trying to win against one's own.

It is moving to encounter a man whose heart is sensitive enough to cheer for each child on a basketball court, but what if we could be like this man in all arenas? What if our default position were to be for each other instead of against each other? What if we could rise above our baser instincts? As it stands, we are automatically suspicious of others, especially those who identify with circles other than our own.

Political sport

Of course, there are arenas of life that are a bit more serious and profound than the high school gym, I think. The ideals that divide our nation politically, ideals concerning marriage, immigration, and race relations, just to name a few, have much greater, more widespread consequences than those of a junior varsity basketball game, don't they? In extreme cases, political decisions are matters of life and death. In such serious arenas, is it possible to be for all sides? Can we simply treat politics like a game in which everyone's effort is as worthy as the next? Most of us would instinctively say, "No. Of course not." We know that these issues are far too important to be treated like a game. Why is it, then, that our society has allowed the political arena to become so much like that of a sporting event?

Our political parties have team colors and mascots. When political opponents line up for debate, people in the audience hold up not so witty banners that attempt to defame the other side. Just like the hometown crowd who would never jeer at a group of innocent teenagers on any other occasion than game night, members of each side have already determined before the first word is said that they want nothing more than to see their side crush and perhaps even embarrass the opponents. We then return time and again to the YouTube highlights to watch that "big hit" one politician delivered to the other, and happily share it all over social media to multiply the humiliation.

In such a climate, politics becomes less and less about finding the best path forward for our nation and more about putting points on the board. I must admit that there have been times in the past when a politician I did not favor made a blunder and I reveled in this person's public embarrassment. I watched with guilty delight while the politician struggled in futility to climb out of the hole he or she had created. And the media makes big bucks on the click bait the modern pillory brings. It is as if we have lost sight of our nation's prosperity and have instead focused our efforts on defaming and defeating the other side.

Words are more than words

The political arena is filled with enemy language, as if we are not simply citizens with varying opinions on how to care for our nation but bitter enemies somehow foreign to one another. It begins with referring to the opposing political party or persons as "them" and "they." Soon the politicians begin to enumerate how "we" are not like "them," and how "they" want to destroy this country. *Destroy* belongs to the vocabulary of war, the language we use to describe what combatants aim to do to our way of life.

Often, we hear that various communities within our own nation, communities composed of citizens just like us, want to "destroy," dismantle," "degrade," and "demolish" our way of life? Why are we using this sort of language in politics? When did it become acceptable to use the same terminology for terrorists and fellow citizens who have a different perspective? Certainly there are times when using strong language is necessary to gain others' attention. Perhaps there are occasions when the language of war is appropriate. We cannot pretend that none of our issues are so serious as to have long term consequences if one side succeeds over the other in implementing its vision.

When we discuss issues wrapped in moral decision-making, we may want to ensure our words strongly affirm our position. When the stakes are high, we may choose to take a firm stand, but if we look to the news and the continued political conversation, we may easily note that such harsh language is not reserved for the gravest discussions but used liberally without much regard to the issue at hand. Certainly this is not a new phenomenon. Slander in politics is probably as old as time. It is certainly as old as American politics:

Jefferson's camp accused President Adams of having a "hideous hermaphroditical character, which has neither the force and firmness of a man, nor the gentleness and sensibility of a woman."

In return, Adams' men called Vice President Jefferson "a mean-spirited, low-lived fellow, the son of a half-breed Indian squaw, sired by a Virginia mulatto father." [ix]

Enemy language is devastatingly effective, not to solve our issues, but to shape the way we think.

Words mold us. We think in words, and when we limit our pool of references for the other side to enemy language, we will soon perceive it as such. When we adopt enemy language to describe those who are not like us, our words will not only shape how we treat the other, but also how the other will react to us. When those on the other side know we think so little of them, they are likely to become suspicious of us. Prejudice breeds more prejudice.

In a society as diverse as ours, preexisting differences are already sufficient to cause fragmentation in our society. When leaders can manipulate these differences to shape our opinions, using only partial truths about other groups, citizens often feel underrepresented and more anxious about encountering each other. When our political leaders engage in rhetoric that pits one group's ideals against another's, this technique shapes the public consciousness, often without the general public's being able to discern the truth because it lacks the resources to evaluate properly the ideas and opinions that shape the way we think:

Developed Western societies are characteristically pluralistic, with diverse and often competing interests that engender fragmentation and its accompanying dangers. Organized and well-financed special interest groups can dominate public rhetoric for or against a proposal. By contrast, the majority of relatively disinterested private citizens typically lack the organization and resources necessary for strong self-awareness as members of a public. Although as vested in the resolution of public problems as the most entrenched lobbyist, their inability to mount a rhetorical counteroffensive on behalf of their commanding interests can make average citizens appear detached from the outcome of public deliberation. Consequently, the dominant voices that seem to mold public opinion are less those of citizens engaged in public deliberation than those of elites who possess access to the forums that court public support, bankroll political candidates, and decide public policy...The pervasive roll of the media in Western political processes further complicates the problematic relationship of discourse to public opinion.[x]

If our leaders have such control, can we ever hope for such devastating rhetoric to end? I think so, but it is going to take a conscious, concerted effort from everyday citizens working together to combat the resources elites have to spin the conversation. However, before we can discuss this solution further, let us first consider what is at stake a little more. This is not just an individual issue toward which one person decides whether or not to do better. Until large groups decide to band together, the effects of enemy language will continue to have wide and systemic effects on our nation.

Consequences

With the real hostility that exists in our nation, we can easily allow distrust to define all interactions with others. Take, for example, an encounter between persons of differing races, such as the all-too-often disastrous encounters between white police officers and black citizens:

Two normal individuals enter a situation in which predefined expectations cause each person to feel threatened by the other. Clear heads often do not prevail. Instead, past references used to describe the other cloud the minds of each individual. In fear, each person, whether knowingly or not, bristles at the other, showing a level of hostility that need not be inherent to such situations, a level of hostility the other will detect and to which he or she will react.

What if, when we recognize the hostility in others, we do not simply assume the worst, but recognize the problem we all share? Perhaps the other is not filled with hate or looking for a fight, but is reacting in fear because of the hate he or she assumes in us as portrayed by the media? What if two otherwise beloved individuals of their own respective communities find themselves in a hostile situation because *all of us* have created an atmosphere of fear through our constant use of enemy language. When we are conditioned to think of the other as an enemy, any encounter with the other will more than likely engage the basic fight or flight response, which often ends disastrously, no matter which option the one feeling threatened decides to take. Both are natural responses, but both responses often end in violence. As we have seen time and again in recent interactions between black citizens and white officers, if one decides to fight or run, chances are that someone is going to lose his or her freedom, and maybe even a life.

Less than human

When we participate in any discussion about an opposing side's use of degrading language, we contribute to the systemic problem of distrust. It is no wonder we now view ourselves as part of a culture war. When we use hostile language, we create a mental willingness to win at all costs because we effectively devalue the other through enemy language. We deny their humanity in our own minds.

> *What all stereotyping has in common, whether it is a product of politics, religion, nationalism, or other forces, is an effort to dehumanize, to erase individuality, to prevent us from looking someone in the eye and learning their name. The consequence is to create a culture of indifference that empathy finds difficult to penetrate.*
> xi

The same language that leads to tension in the public square is also used to justify treating others disrespectfully in public. Many are willing to debase themselves by using terms such as "fool," "idiot," "moron," and the like because through such words, they no longer have to recognize the target of their defamation as human. Diminishing the humanity of any group ultimately robs us all of our inherent dignity. Meanwhile, each side persistently blames the other for lack of cooperation.

With such name-calling, political bipartisanship seems more and more impossible. Race relations remain strained in the public sphere. Religious monikers have become slanderous descriptions. Almost anything that can be used to describe a person is now a dividing line, and there is no insult too nasty. Some have become so callous, so willing to insult the other side, that they would attempt to devalue them by comparing them to people with disabilities, as if the disable, too, are somehow less human. I have come to despise the terms *libtard* and *conservatard*.

Whom can we blame?

So how do we combat the issue?

Enemy language is a tool of enemy making, and the art of enemy making is the ability to create in others a lack of worth. When we can take our focus off others' human worth, we can go to any lengths to crush their efforts or even their very person in order to have our way in shaping the world as we wish to see it. It is in places we should least tolerate such tactics that we use them the most, the sphere of politics, the place where we choose the fate of our nation and, consequently, each other.

The political sphere is an arena with one of the most influential pulls on the public consciousness. We do not all relate to each other's ethnic celebrations. We do not all share in each other's family circles. We do not all participate in each other's faiths. Yet we all, simply by living within this country's borders, find ourselves politically involved with one another. If we choose, therefore, to make this an arena of animosity, we will have a big war to fight.

We should make no mistake; creating this war has become big business. It has become commonplace for a candidate's campaign to create full-time jobs requiring staffers to spend the entire political season attempting to unearth skeletons to discredit and humiliate the opponent, or worse, to malign someone related to the opponent who never volunteered for the public spotlight, much less the microscope, and the media is all too willing to expose these wounds for all to see.

Sadly, the public has become complicit in its eagerness to consume the most private details with little regard for modesty or the Golden Rule. Politics practiced in such a way has made a public willing to define a person by the worst thing he or she has ever done and an unwillingness to forgive others or celebrate the best in them.

Our politicians are not all to blame, not by a long shot. Just like businesses that wish to thrive, the success of the politician is about giving the people what they want. Just as businesses hire public relations firms to tell them what sells, politicians hire public relations firms to tell them what gets votes. Politicians don't simply shape our thoughts, nor do they simply share in the way we think, but *they also respond to the way we think*. It is a cycle. If the public consciousness responds to hateful language, fear mongering, and battle lines, that is what we will get from our leaders. We say, "Sex sells."

Hate seems to be pretty marketable as well.

If there is to be any hope for our nation, change must begin on a much more basic level. It has to happen in everyday life. It has to start before it ever reaches the political stages. We, the people, must demand respect and civility from one another, but in order to demand it, we must first give it. If we can hold ourselves to these standards, then, and only then, can we tell our politicians that we will stand for nothing less than civility towards all people. How can our standing up for what is right be effective on the world stage? It is simple supply and demand. Only when we choose to respond to nothing less than respect will we gain leaders willing to be fully respectful. It will then not only be the right thing to do, but the pragmatic thing as well.

Shifting Our Focus

Eighty-one percent of Americans believe we are more divided as a nation than ever before and hold little hope for any measure of meaningful reconciliation in the future.[xii] In light of our disagreements, many politicize their ideals and dehumanize any person or group offering a different opinion. This trend has created an "us versus them" mentality that transforms neighbors into enemies based merely upon a superficial understanding of what they are for or against, rather than the deeper reasons why they think and feel as they do. So, what can we do to change this? How do we stop the cycle of enemy language?

Without bias or blame, our team took an intimately transparent look into the lives and stories of several subjects who represent the diverse sides of issues surrounding race, immigration, and marriage, just as a sample of the numerous issues we fight over every day. It is our hope that by telling these ordinary, yet seldom discussed stories, we may reintroduce the human element as the antidote to our culture wars. If stereotypes and prejudice dehumanize the other, perhaps the cure is re-humanization.

Our hope is to show something beneath the surface of the points and counterpoints that bombard us through various media avenues. If we have not come up with an effective argument to silence the other by now, it seems that no amount of debate is likely to do much to change the animosity of either side towards the other. In fact, if current trends continue, we will only further polarize ourselves from one another.

Throughout this project we have allowed people from each side to make their case in the way they wish to do so; we have not asked them to convince us of anything. We already know the arguments, as well as how they are made. We spend whole political seasons hearing from proponents of each side. We know our responses as well. We also know why we already agree or disagree. What we want to explore is something deeper. We are not asking what but why. Our goal is not to promote one side over the other; instead, we present our subjects' sincere thoughts in an effort to underscore our common humanity. Our hope is not that those in our audience will change their minds about the issues necessarily, but that they will experience a change of heart toward those with whom they disagree.

The only questions we want answered are these: After giving an honest reading to the following stories, how do you want to respond, even in light of disagreement? Is it possible to be compassionate in the midst of controversy? Can you imagine yourself getting to know the other and having an honest, open, and even vulnerable conversation about how we might move forward despite our differences? Our goal is modest. We want to take one step, a first step, in the right direction, a step toward compassion and civility.

Keep the opinion; leave the hate

Showing kindness and compassion does not have to mean forfeiting ideals. That man sitting near my mother that Friday night knew the game had to end with one team's winning and one team's losing. I do not believe that everything in politics has to be polarized, but, in the end, there will be consequences we all must face, and some of those will be less than agreeable to some. That is just reality.

We cannot control this, but what we can control is how we face this reality. We have tried treating politics like a game. We have tried dehumanizing our neighbors in order to defeat them. The results of such have proved ineffective. Some may have succeeded in defeating the others' optimism and cooperative spirit, but we have not succeeded in bettering our nation. We feel more divided than ever. Was that the result we were looking for?

What we wanted was to see our ideals win on the public stage, but very few Americans on either side feel that they are really winning. Perhaps we are doing this wrong. Many would argue that we have seen the war on drugs fail. Many would argue that we have seen the war on poverty fail. Maybe some problems simply cannot be fixed by war. Perhaps it is time to surrender our culture wars altogether and opt for solutions that do not aim to destroy those we find in the wrong.

Our Challenge

Everyone who reads the following pages will encounter a subject who presents a disagreeable view, at least for those who have an opinion on our nation's most controversial issues. If engaging in a conversation that requires both sides to listen is too much to ask, we will be stuck on our current path, and face a bleak future. If we care enough for our nation and even our world to admit we have a problem, can we spend some time simply considering the merits of civility and compassion in the public square? If we can set aside our opinions for one moment and allow the other to talk, we may pick them back up when we are finished and learn that while our fundamental ideals may remain, we do not want to use them as an excuse to hurt anyone. This was our belief in initiating this process. Now that we have heard stories from all sides, that belief is even stronger.

Our subjects

Representing both sides of the immigration debate are Nico and Dalila, an undocumented Hispanic couple, and Chuck and Kathy, a white, working class couple. Nico and Dalila never imagined how difficult life could be when they dreamed of coming to America, but after starting a family in the U.S., they constantly confront the severity of their situation, as one wrong encounter with the law could tear their family apart. Their biggest dream is to be real contributors to their community if only they could leave the shadows.

Chuck and Kathy's dreams came crashing down when the multimillion-dollar construction business they had built from nothing could no longer compete with rising undocumented competition. They do not blame undocumented workers for seeking a better life, but they desire a better system in which members of no group are under threat of losing their dream for another to have theirs.

Representing the two sides of marriage, we explore the lives of Megan and Desiree and Drew and Mandy. Striving to navigate their lives gracefully as a gay married couple who deeply desires to remain an active part of the Christian community, Megan and Desiree want others to know they respect convictions, even when those convictions lead others to believe differently. Still, this couple hopes disagreement never means that any member of society should be treated with anything less than compassion and civility.

After dealing with depression, miscarriage, and infertility, Drew and Mandy know what it is like to have honest struggles in life and faith. Today, this pastor and pastor's wife hold great gratitude for the traditional faith that brought them through their struggles and have consequently dedicated their lives to ever growing obedience. Through it all, they have come to see their faith, not as something to impose upon others, but as a gift to offer those looking for a meaningful life.

Finally, as we consider racial tensions, we gain a perspective of hope for all who feel torn in the various culture wars of our day. Our discussion of race is not really about presenting two sides, as in the case of immigration and marriage, but about hope in the midst of controversy. Racism in any form directed towards any ethnicity is obviously wrong. Instead of exploring race as a means to present diverse, yet meaningful differences, we will look to one couple as an example of hope for all who experience adversity in any form. Because race is not new to public discourse, those who have lived through past pain and face future challenges can offer much wisdom.

Black American couple Vernon and Portia Jackson use their long history of confronting the struggles and fears engendered by racial discord to share how they have managed to thrive despite an ongoing culture war. At the center of their message is living proof of compassion's success in the midst of a disjointed and confusing world. Hopefully, the wisdom Vernon and Portia share in recounting their struggles will encourage persons who feel hurt and attacked in the crossfire of our cultural disagreements.

Compassion and civility are only the first steps toward healing, but the first steps are the most crucial. What those next steps are, we are not here to share because we have yet to get to a point where we have tried the first step, but what we do know is this: We will never get where we want to go unless we start heading in the right direction. In the end, we may never come to agree, but we may learn to care deeply for one another, nonetheless.

Let's explore the other side.

Section II: Backgrounds

Assumptions are shaped by many factors, including prior experience and learned behaviors. Children are especially influenced by learned behavior as they take note of the postures, references, and general attitudes their parents, teachers, and other influential adults adopt when encountering someone who is "other."

For the child, noticing someone else is different is first a matter of curiosity. Negative bias is introduced when this child perceives a negative attitude in those he or she most often imitates. The child does not become malicious at this point. He or she is simply following a basic rule of survival: *If others in my community recoil from this type of person, thing, or situation, I should too.*[xiii]

If prejudice can be ingrained at such an early age, we might fear that there is little hope of overcoming our prejudices unless we begin by admitting that none of us are immune to receiving or perpetuating, consciously or subconsciously, negative stereotypes. We do, however, have another mechanism in learning about others that may move us beyond learned biases: an uncanny ability to empathize through the vicarious experience of placing ourselves in another's shoes. When we have the opportunity to learn of others through hearing their stories and placing ourselves in their shoes, learned biases are diminished if not destroyed, and we learn, instead, to care.

In July 2011, The Greater Good Science Center, based at the University of California, Berkley reported on a study published the month prior in *The Journal of Personality and Social Psychology*, noting that automatic bias can be significantly reduced through empathy.

For the study, participants were asked to view two similar situations involving one white subject and one black subject. The video presented two scenarios, one in which the black subject was treated unfairly, apparently because of his race, and one in which the white subject navigated the same situations without conflict.

The participants were split into three groups. Members of one group were asked to think about how they thought the black subject felt during the ordeal. Members of the second group were asked to think how they would feel in the same situation as the black subject. A final group was asked to remain objective and never prompted to consider how one might feel in the situation. The first two groups had to empathize, either indirectly or directly, while the third did not. The results were conclusive. Both of the groups asked to empathize demonstrated significantly less bias than the one asked to remain objective. Even more important, other variations of the study showed that those who were asked to think of persons different from themselves showed significant increases in real world interactions with people who were "other."[xiv]

Chapter Three: "Redeeming The Past"

Walking away from expectations

In many ways this could be considered the typical suburban household. American flags fly throughout the neighborhood. People bustle about as they manicure their lawns. Children play games up and down the lane.

The large home is full of movement as the children mill all about. The eldest son, home from college for a short visit, sneaks off to the attached in-law suite for a bit of solitude while the three small foster girls bounce and giggle in the den, but not before he raids the fridge. Cartoons flicker in the background, but the little ones are not paying much attention. It's snack time. The teenage daughter paces in her room, making plans over the phone with friends for the weekend before she has to rush off to work.

The man of the house is the systems technician at a local medical lab. The woman of the house stays home to care for the children and cuts hair in the spare apartment above the garage. They invite our team into their large living room down the hall from the den so that we might have a generally peaceful conversation. The husband and wife run a well organized home. The son is a gentleman and the girls are attentive to their father's instructions. The father gives firm, but loving orders, and the children respond without a second's hesitation. The children's constant laughter denotes that while their foster parents provide discipline and encourage respect, they do not do so at the expense of the children's spirits. Good behavior is not coerced but patiently instilled.

Perhaps the most telling sign of a peaceful home was the children's reaction to five strangers who barged in with loads of equipment. They did not stand quietly in the corner, speaking only when spoken to. Instead, they busily crawled between the crew's legs as if we were family. They were inquisitive about the cameras, lights, and audio equipment. They did not see us as intruders into their normal routine but as potential playmates.

Altogether, these people present the picture of the successful American family. From the oldest to the youngest, everyone has a purpose. They are independent and happy. They exist as that increasingly rare instance of the intact family that has its collective act together in this turbulent society, and according to the man of the house, this family credits much of its success to a tradition of teaching resilience, diligence, self-discipline, and hard work. The family feels free to dream big, and they more often than not see their dreams come true. They live what many would call the American Dream.

We have all met this family before, right? Assiduous, tenacious, cohesive, successful, and capable of dreaming big despite the struggles around them, and they are black: "We're hard workers. We believe in the Lord. We believe in America," Vernon tells us. Why does the color of their skin matter? It shouldn't. No one should be surprised to see a stable and successful black family such as the Jacksons, but as Vernon explains, many did not have such expectations for him and, surprisingly, even after years of success, many still do not.

A few moments of conversation are enough to reveal the confident, determined man Vernon has become, but even by Vernon's own admission, his success was not always guaranteed. In fact, one event almost stole Vernon's courage to be who he wanted to be. Before he could share this event, he had to leave the room to compose himself. Tearfully, he removed his microphone and disappeared.

May Day

"May Day is coming! May Day is coming!" Every year

as May 1 approached, the warning of "May Day" would spread through the black neighborhoods of Baltimore. "It was well known," Vernon told us, "there was going to be confrontation." According to Vernon, there was an expectation that many of the white community would use this holiday as a chance to terrorize any black person who dared show his or her face in public. It had become a favorite pastime, and on May 1, 1973, Vernon was one group's means of celebrating this tradition.

"Usually, the fights took place at night," Vernon said. During the day, Vernon, along with his family and friends, could see white men and boys up the hill posturing and getting ready for the night's activities, but no one, so many in his community thought, was foolish enough to act in the day time, especially since a police station was located directly in between the neighborhoods.

"No one expected things to kick off that early, and Mom needed things from the store, so she sent me to the A&P. The A&P was kind of midway between where the whites lived and where the blacks lived," Vernon explained. He was able to make it in and out of the store without a problem, but when he neared the police station on his walk home, a car out of nowhere sped in front of him and slammed on the brakes, cutting him off when he tried to cross the street. One after another, men with sticks and dogs began to climb out.

"I knew what was about to happen. The first thing they said was, 'Get that nigger!'" Vernon remembers that the initial contact was not that physically painful, just some pushing and shoving. He was in a fairly open space, an old lot used for little more than parking from time to time. Able to dodge most of the initial barrage, Vernon told us he was more frightened than hurt by the first few hits, but when he was finally struck with a stick, he knew the situation was serious. "Pain shot through my left arm," Vernon paused for a moment and held the area of his arm where he was struck. He grimaced, as if he were feeling the pain all over again. We waited in horror before he returned to the story.

After the first real blow, another car stopped and the men who got out were carrying miniature bats from Oriole Stadium. Some brought real bats as well. Now that there were so many attackers, Vernon was encircled. He knew he could not dodge the next wave of attack: "They started hitting me kind of soft at first, poking and pushing, so I started running and dodging and trying to make a hole and get away. I knew the police station was just across the fence. I felt like if I made it that far the police would help." After what seemed like several minutes of dodging some blows while taking some others, Vernon spotted a smaller boy among the group and knew this boy would be the weak link in the blockade. "I could run through him. I broke the line where he was and ran onto the lawn where the police department was." The brutal gang would have to leave him alone now…or so he thought.

Terror filled him all over again when Vernon, realizing his escape had only angered and provoked his attackers further, saw the gang do the unthinkable. Furious, they pursued him onto the police station lawn. "I can remember bats and sticks just hitting me. One guy had his dog by the collar and he would shake the dog and push the dog into my stomach and it would bite. He kept saying, 'Make him feel it.' I kept thinking, the police have to know I'm here. They have to know."

One of the last things Vernon felt was his face opening in response to a hit and warm blood rushing from the wound. He could smell his own blood now. While he lay on his back, he tilted his head to see if the police were coming out of the station to help. Barely conscious with blood running into his eyes, he could see several policemen watching in what seemed to be amusement from a window. "Something died inside of me. Something really, really broke. I went numb. I could feel the punches, but nothing mattered anymore. I could feel the sticks, feel the hits, smell my blood. I felt everything, but there was nothing I could do about it, and the hope of survival was gone because they weren't saying, 'Help that boy.' They were saying, 'Get him.'" Vernon was twelve years old.

Injustice after injustice

According to Vernon, the rest of the altercation was really a blur. He moved in and out of consciousness, but the attack had gone on long enough for someone from his neighborhood to notice the commotion and call for help. His father and brother, both very large and strong men, broke through the crowd and fought their way to Vernon. Even Vernon's 5'1" mother got involved. Vernon felt someone grab his arm and pull him away from it all. It was then that some of the police officers came out and disbanded the fight.

After the paramedics arrived and bandaged him, the police took Vernon and his mother on a ride to "find those responsible." Even though they had seen the real culprits themselves, the officers drove Vernon and his mother up and down the black neighborhoods, asking him to identify anyone he could recognize as part of the "gang" that had attacked him. They remained in his own neighborhood, never taking him up the hill to the white neighborhood from which the mob had come. Vernon was confused at first, but his mother knew what was going on, and she motioned for her son to stay quiet until they could get out the car and go to the hospital, where he received many stitches for his wounds. Vernon endured the rest of that absurd manhunt silently while wracked with pain in the back seat of the squad car. No one was ever arrested for the assault on Vernon that day.

Hating hatred

In the days after, Vernon kept asking himself, "Why me?" He could make no sense of what had happened. What twelve-year-old child could? Vernon now remembers that confused, emotionally numbed child and considers how he was nearly lost that day. He was almost consumed by his rage. He could have become another angry, young, black man who lashed out against a society that, as far as he knew, hated him. Yet, as statistics affirm all too well, this would most likely have ended with Vernon in the prison system and the world around him telling him he had no one to blame but himself.

Racism urged Vernon to return hate with hate, but the intervention of one man kept the hate poured upon Vernon from becoming the venom that could have so easily and almost justifiably infected him with racism: "The church that we grew up in was white and black. They believed in anointing and laying on hands. Mr. Marvin Hush was white. He came in and got his oil. He put it on my head, and he prayed for me and for complete healing." Vernon paused from his story again, and he shook his head, as if he still couldn't quite believe it. "I remember looking at Mr. Hush. He was white, and he was crying, as if to say, 'Nobody should ever have to go through this.' I can remember his prayer: 'Just correct the wrongs. Correct the wrongs. Correct the wrongs.' He said, 'correct the wrongs' so many times in that prayer. I think that was the point that made me fight racism and not white people."

This, according to Vernon, was the moment when he was able to think more clearly about what was going on around him. It was not simply "white people" who did this to him. He had a community of white people surrounding him every Sunday, and they had never shown him anything but love and acceptance. Now, they showed him that what had happened was inexcusable. It was unjust. And they cried and sought justice along with his family.

Vernon came to the conclusion that his attackers were a particular group of white people who were themselves deeply broken. Something in their lives made them capable of hating an innocent boy simply because of his skin color, and that hate made them capable of attacking a twelve-year-old carrying groceries for his mother, five loaves of bread to be precise, five loaves that never made it to the house. It was this hate that Vernon wanted to destroy, not the people.

This is where Vernon has chosen to live, and no matter what comes his way, this experience has made his determination to fight hate that much stronger. After telling us his story, he wiped the tears from his eyes and described the sort of strength he developed from all of this: "You can't hate me more than I love you." This is his message, one some might see as too idealistic, but Vernon told us, "Sometimes, we need to plant a seed and expect it to grow." Vernon forgives and expects forgiveness to spread in return. Vernon hopes and expects hope to spread in return. Vernon loves and expects love to spread in return. Vernon dreams and expects those dreams to grow in return.

Our team listened to Vernon's story in dismay. Perhaps we were not surprised, especially with the current reprisal of overt racial violence we see today, but what did surprise us was Vernon's conclusion. He does not deny the issue is real, nor does he believe it can be dismissed. He knows that forgiveness does not justify hate. But even in light of his own experience, he prefers to hold on to hope. When Vernon continued to speak, we held our breath in anticipation. We realized we had just discovered something and someone special, but we weren't quite sure how all of this would unfold.

Choosing Vernon

It was after this story that we realized Vernon would not be another subject in our project or a representative of "his side." Instead, he would be a voice of wisdom. While all our subjects shared moments of great wisdom, Vernon was speaking from a unique place. For all our other subjects, their stories of facing cultural war were still raw and still in progress. Vernon and Portia still live within the confines of what it means to be black in America, but they have lived in this place for decades and have developed a philosophy for facing adversity, a philosophy we want all people to hear, no matter what adversity they face.

Though our team quickly realized Vernon had an important message for our nation, we knew people would want to know him, even beyond his compelling story of victimization, before they could appreciate his perspective. People would want to know, not only about the twelve-year-old who had survived, but also the man who was now using his story as strength to help others.

Taking advice from a stranger is neither common nor prudent. The problem is that Vernon is a modest man who tells his story with a humility that can impede the impact of the story in which he is the hero. To discover who Vernon is, we need only look to his wife. Portia's undying confidence in her husband is a testimony far richer than that which Vernon could tell of himself. Portia is a woman with immense vision for sharing love with others, and nothing could obscure that dream. Her decision to trust Vernon with her dream speaks volumes of this man. Though the old expression says, "Behind every great man, is a great woman," in this instance it would be better to say, "*Beside* every great man, is a great woman." Vernon and Portia live their dream together.

Portia grew up in Philadelphia with her mother, father, and her mentally handicapped, non-verbal brother, as well as a constant flow of people in need who were brought in as family. Her neighborhood was a rough Philadelphia ghetto, and, as part of a community pushed to the margins of public concern, the family experienced poverty. Even with some adversity, Portia remembers her childhood and neighborhood very positively: "Our ghetto was not the same as the ghettos that are in existence today," she said. "People had concern for one another, love for one another."

Despite her impoverished conditions, Portia describes life in Philadelphia as quite exciting and full: "My mother and father did not limit any of my experiences and opportunities. They exposed me to everything. My dad was really aggressive about life and learning." Even though they did not have much money, Portia's parents knew how to expose their children to culture.

While she might not have realized it at the time, her father's push for diverse cultural experience kept her from the assumption that the ghetto was it. Portia knew there was more to life than her limited, local experiences exposed because her father took the time to show her. Portia's parents did not allow no money to equate with no experiences. Portia's belief in possibilities flourished because of her father's efforts. Portia's hope, however, did not drive her to seek what most of us consider success. She did not dream simply of having that which she didn't already have, especially money. Her father's impact was much more profound. Portia dreamed of having and sharing more of what her parents were already providing: compassion and direction.

Compounded with her father's ability to reveal the possibilities life has to offer was a profound sense of the limitless potential of love for others could accomplish. Portia's mother was the driving force behind this perspective. While her father loved cultural experience, Portia mother was passionate about people. Because she knew that if she didn't help others in their impoverished community, especially children whose families might be unable to support the home, the community would lose them, Portia's mother, like others in their neighborhood, took in children, to feed, clothe, and adopt.

When a new need arose, Portia's mother would make a way: "My mother would say, 'Just add another plate to the table. There's plenty of food.' Even though there may not have been enough food, she always divvied it up so we all had some." As a result, Portia grew up with many, many "brothers and sisters" in a home always open to others.

The American ideal of creating the perfect nuclear home with a mother, a father, and 2.5 children while moving towards the dream of an empty nest and quiet retirement never captured Portia's imagination. Today, Portia's immediate family is an intact, loving, and connected family, but this does not define the boundaries of her home. Old enough to be a grandmother, Portia parents an open family teeming with children who come in and out of the home. The Jacksons are lifelong foster parents who provide a stable family for those who do not have a family of their own.

The combined influence of her parents has led Portia to develop a beautiful, alternative type of family, one that is large but always open for growth, one always ready to offer love without an invitation: "I grew up with a lot of brothers and sisters that weren't blood. To me they were just like blood, just like family. As a matter of fact, we sometimes called them "Uncle," "Aunt," "cousin." Though their biological children are now adults, Vernon and Portia still have little ones living in their home. A lifestyle many might consider sacrificial, the Jacksons consider normal.

For Portia, it was important that her children maintain a sense of these blurred lines: "Even my children today, they say to me, 'Mom, are they *really* our cousins, or are they just kind of make believe?'" Portia's response teaches her children that for their family, this question doesn't really have meaning. Smiling, Portia told us how she always responds: "Well, they're cousins, you know. Period." Portia continues, "That's pretty much the way I grew up." That legacy will continue if Portia has any say.

A woman who sees love as a force that tears down the limited imaginations of what family and love can be, Portia is a testament to the man she chose to marry. While Portia was never limited in what she believed possible for her own life, she understood that others may not find the ability to dream big easy. She knew who she wanted to be, and she believed the best way to be that person was to remain single. Then she met Vernon, a man who convinced her she could be married and still achieve her dreams.

"When I met him, I didn't think that I could meet someone like him. I was not really anxious to get married. But, when he proposed to me, he said, 'You can be whatever you want to be. I'm not going to shackle you down.'" Portia knew words are not the same as actions. It was important for her to find a man who not only loved her, but who also dreamed like her, loved like her, and had room in his heart for others in need.

She needed a man who, as she put it, "would never meet a stranger, that would allow someone to come into our home and just be if they needed to be." Portia introduced Vernon to two of her family's adopted children on their first date to see how he would handle having others in the midst of their relationship. Without hesitation, Vernon took them all out to eat, paid, and spent time getting to know all of them, not just Portia.

By the time Vernon proposed, Portia knew Vernon meant what he said when he promised she could pursue her dreams of loving without limits. If Portia wanted to dream about helping others, he was more than happy not just to watch, but to enable and participate. The home in which they now reside is proof that Portia's dream of helping others has become a reality.

While we stood in the driveway after one of our interviews, Vernon looked back at his house and said, "Well, it looks lived in," and it did, but not in worn way. We could simply see the physical marks of a home well used and still useful. As a final testament to her husband's love and character, Portia told us about how and why the in-law suite was added: "When we moved to this house, it was just big enough for our family." When her mother and father reached an age at which they needed assistance, Portia told us that, without hesitation, Vernon rose to the occasion: "He built an in-law suite and made them comfortable." They remained there until Portia's mother passed. To remove himself from the memories, Portia's father moved out, but Portia is forever grateful that her husband was willing to house the couple who first taught her how to grow a home for the needs of others: "So, that's the type of man I married, and I'm grateful to have him."

A legacy of hope

The fourth of five children, four boys and one girl, Vernon was born in Baltimore, Maryland in 1961. With such a large family, it was necessary for his father to work two jobs while his mother stayed home to look after everyone. At times, things were tough for the family. Occasionally, when Vernon's father was between jobs, the family went without electricity.

"Dad made poverty fun. He would put a tent in the basement and open the windows to prevent dangerous fumes. We had a Coleman heater." After the heater warmed the tent, all the children would climb inside. "That's where we would cook and eat," he added. Through the lean times, as well as the more prosperous ones, Vernon's mother made sure the family stayed in order. Though it was not always easy, she raised her children under strict rules, and, as Vernon told us repeatedly, ensured the children "made the best of things, made the right decisions, and lived in a way that would be pleasing to God."

While his mother was trying her best to show Vernon the value of a virtuous life, his older brothers were teaching Vernon self-defense. Perhaps the two lessons were not that opposed to one another considering the circumstances. Vernon remembers times in Baltimore when everyone had to fight to survive, and without good grounding, children could easily lose their way. Learning to protect one's self could also be used for less than noble purposes: "If you didn't believe in who you were, if you didn't know where you were going, it was easy to get in trouble."

Once older, Vernon could have used his voice, which rolls like thunder, and his size to intimidate, but a voice of reason constantly whispered in his ear: "My parents made sure that our goals were on the right track. We all ended up in a better place because of our upbringing and were able to make strong and right decisions and stay true to our values," Vernon explained.

While Vernon's father obscured their poverty with fun, Vernon's mother kept the family grounded. Playing the realist in difficult circumstances could have made Vernon's mother a pessimist, but her responsibilities never broke her spirit: "My mother has rose colored glasses permanently fixed on her spirit, and she sees the best in everything and everybody. She brightens up every room she is in." Considering her son's fate and the authorities' compliance on that terrible May Day in 1973, it is surprising that she never gave up herself.

****

Vernon and Portia are testimonies to the long road. In a time when we crave instant results and quick remedies, Vernon and Portia demonstrate the lasting power of legacy. What we begin today in our children, we can never fully understand until they are grown and have children and grandchildren of their own. Each commitment made to approach our fellow man with dignity and respect will produce a gradual return. Opposition meets us every day, and, as Vernon's story illustrates, holds the power to threaten our very existence, but it can be overcome. While so many today are losing hope, the Jacksons' lives exemplify the virtue of long-suffering.

Presently, Vernon's mother is in poor health, but, according to Vernon, her spirit is strong. When she must visit the hospital, she remains mindful of the doctors' and nurses' needs, and she makes sure to put a smile on their faces when they enter her room. She worked in a nursing home for years herself, and she remembers the toll taking care of the elderly can take; therefore, she has made it her duty to care for those who care for her.

Even as her health fades, her legacy grows stronger in her son. Her perseverance, never divorced from compassion, is not something we see every day, but we do see it in Vernon. An attitude of getting the job done no matter how bad things are is too often coupled with an attitude of getting the job done no matter whom you might run over on the way. Vernon's mother's path is much narrower. Never giving up is a hard road to walk in the first place, but joining that road with the directive never to harm another is a road few people wish to walk. For Vernon, however, having such a focus is crucial: "Make the right decisions and carve the right road for yourselves and those who will follow you. It is important to cut a path that's going in the right direction, because there is a lot of life that goes in the wrong direction."

After speaking of his mother's legacy for a while, Portia interjected to make sure we understood that Vernon embodies his mother's convictions: "He always looks for the good in others and other things, and I have learned how to do that from him. My mother and father were largely realists and somewhat pessimistic. My father will look at things very closely before he takes a leap of faith, Vernon looks at things and sees things that aren't there because his mother and father were the type of people that look at things and see everything that could be there, and that's the difference." Whether one is raised a pragmatist like Portia or an idealist like Vernon, one can always live for the benefit of others.

It is hard to imagine the fusion of virtues that exist in the marriage between Portia and Vernon. Their story melts stereotypes, hate, and the sense of otherness, and that is why we had to showcase their family.

Chapter Four: "We Dream"

If I were to close my eyes and forget who was speaking, I am not sure I would be able to distinguish the dreams expressed by the Venturas and the Padgetts. Their dreams, the kind of dreams only the poor can have, dreams of what they can only imagine is "normal," both emanate from a place of despair.

Only the poor dream of having that which most middle class Americans take for granted, visions that begin simply with the desire for stability and security, a dream that both families often summed up in the word *home*. Even with such common dreams and modest beginnings, these families find themselves on opposite ends of the volatile immigration debate.

Chuck and Nico aren't vocal advocates for opposing sides of the debate. They haven't the luxury of pontificating the pros and cons of immigration. Unlike many who engage in the immigration debate, Chuck and Nico live in the midst of what immigration means in America.

For Chuck Padgett, the state of immigration in America has meant losing much of what he had dreamed of having because the government lacked control over undocumented workers who never had to pay into the system to which Chuck's business was held accountable and thereby made fair competition with companies using undocumented workers impossible.

Nico, on the other hand, is an undocumented worker. He came to the United States hoping to participate in the job market, but he never dreamed this would mean taking from those already here. The American Dream as it was explained to him offered everyone opportunity. Money was here for the taking. Now that he has made his way to America, he, too, understands the lack of control the government has over a system that allowed him to find a job, marry, and have children, only to find out that this same system denies the family he was allowed to build peace and security at home because the constant fear of deportation overshadows them. Though Chuck and Nico have experienced the immigration issue from opposite sides, everything they have done came from a kindred hope to provide for those they love.

Childhood dreams

The Padgetts

Chuck and Kathy fell in love because, as they often said, they simply understood each other. They both knew what it was like to look with longing at the world around them and see white picket fences, well-groomed lawns, and families who moved in and out of suburban homes with what seemed to be great ease.

Kathy states, "Growing up, we did not have a normal life." When asked to describe what she meant by "normal," Kathy spoke at length about the picturesque American neighborhoods where life was a joy to live, the lives of the television families she watched and admired as a child when she had the luxury of electricity. Kathy grew up with a lot of cares. She knew life was not all it could be.

Perhaps it would have been better if she had never experienced what she felt to be normal, if she could have assumed that life as she knew was as good as it gets. Kathy, however, knew what it was like to have a comfortable life, not only from what she saw on television, but also from her own experience when she was very small. Her father had owned his own business and had done fairly well in the beginning.

For a while, they did exchange the normal Christmas and birthday gifts, and they could take family vacations, but these ended when Kathy was very young. After her father lost his business, he found employment driving trucks for a while and eventually attempted to operate a truck stop.

Unfortunately, all of his money went into keeping the business afloat, even at the cost of his family's home life. From the age of seven, Kathy lived in poverty: "It was not a clean environment to live in. My dad just kind of brought home any stranger that needed a place to stay. So, you never knew who you were going to wake up in the same house with." Kathy had four older siblings, all brothers, but three were already out of the home when Kathy was small. Kathy and the brother closest to her age grew close because they went through a lot together.

There were times when home for Kathy's family was nothing more than a camper outside of her dad's failing business. They often had no electricity or running water, and when they did have the occasional good fortune to live in an actual house, her bedroom was her safe place. It was here, alone in her room, that Kathy dreamed of a future home in which every room would provide peace and a sense of stability. While other children's impossible dreams involved becoming a princess, Kathy's involved a home and life in suburbia. Outside her room, Kathy confronted something much different: "The things I saw as a child, I should have never saw."

There was a lot of drinking in her home. With her father's encouragement, Kathy had her first drink when she was nine, but it was not simply a sip. She got drunk at her father's side. He instructed her to go straight to bed without speaking to her mother, "It's a miracle I'm not an alcoholic," Kathy said. She says her father was not a bad man, but he wanted the children to drink, because "that meant it was okay for him to drink."

Kathy grew up embarrassed about where she lived, which was so deep in the woods that her bus driver convinced her to walk to the next home over to be picked up, which she happily agreed to since it meant her friends would not see her house. When she began to go out, she met her dates in town. She was also embarrassed about her possessions. She never had the latest cloths. In fact, all she wore was hand-me-downs.

While the other kids were showing off their "white boots and bell bottom jeans," Kathy was wearing someone else's "out-of-date polyester."

In so many ways, Kathy's saving grace was her mother. "She was our rock," Kathy said more than once. When Kathy's mother got a job at a Christian school, she was able to get Kathy in. Kathy was much more at home at the new school because the other children also often wore hand-me-downs. Plus, by this time, Kathy had gotten her own job and bought herself two pair of name brand jeans. She constantly washed them so that no one would know she only had the two.

Kathy's mother, a devout Christian, was always in church. She encouraged her children to come with her, but most often they, lacking interest, stayed home with their father. Still, Kathy knew her mother was praying for them. Kathy's mother never manipulated her with guilt, but her silent devotion to another way of life piqued Kathy's interest. Kathy's mother spent her summers gathering fresh produce, often finding people who had a surplus to give away, and preserving it so that they had something to eat year round. Kathy knew her mother was doing her best, and for Kathy, that was the problem. Kathy wanted more than that for herself. While she never took her mother for granted, she needed to believe she could have a better life.

While Kathy grew up poor, her family remained intact. Chuck, however, came from a broken home. His parents divorced before he was born. At first, Chuck lived with his father, who, like Kathy's, was an alcoholic. Chuck's father loved to fight, and he encouraged Chuck at an early age to fight as well: "My first two years in school, I was probably kicked out four times for fighting."

For Chuck, fighting was harmless enough until the night he saw his father abusing Chuck's step-mother severely: "I remember just being crunched down in the corner of a bedroom just watching." Chuck's face flushed and his voice cracked when he recounted the event. It was a horrible experience for Chuck, and he swore to himself then that he would never lay a finger on a woman. In tears he told us that to this day, he has not. Chuck had to make a conscious effort to adopt a moral stance most people take for granted because of his early life experiences.

After several incidents, Chuck's stepmother left his father, and so did Chuck. His stepmother called his mother and arranged for them to meet. After Chuck was dropped off with his mother, they followed his stepmother to the airport. Chuck did not see her for many years after that night, but he at least knew she was safe. No child should have to imagine a future for which his dream is to avoid beating his wife, but some of us have to begin with smaller dreams than others. If peace in the home is not even a possibility, then it is a mighty dream after all.

Soon after the incident, Chuck's mother gained custody of him, and he lived with her until he was old enough to move out on his own. For a long time, Chuck and his mother lived in a tiny one bedroom, one bath apartment owned by his grandfather. They shared the bed. After some time, however, as Chuck put it, "My mom caught a break." She remarried and had a decent home for twelve years with her new husband. Soon after his mother married this new man, Chuck and one of his childhood friends were walking to his house when they saw a lot of cars lining the street. Everyone in a small town knows that if there is no social event, a collection of people at the house can only mean there has been a death. Chuck rushed inside to find out that his biological father had been killed in a car wreck.

At first, Chuck wanted to feel sorry for himself. All the other kids were learning how to play ball, hunt and fish, and behave on a date from their fathers. Chuck's father had often been absent, and now Chuck knew the absence was final. His mother's new husband, however, soon stepped in and taught Chuck many things, such as hunting, which Chuck still enjoys today.

After Chuck's mother was promoted from waitress to manager at the local Waffle House, she let him work on weekends to earn extra money, but he could not spend it however he liked. She provided the day-to-day items he needed, like clothes and food, but if he wanted a truck, he had to pay for it. At thirteen he began to make the payments on his stepfather's four-wheel drive Dodge pickup with the understanding that once he paid it off at sixteen, it was his. Chuck credits his mother with his tenacity. For many young boys, getting a truck was a luxury, but Chuck saw it, even at thirteen, as a tool to help him work for a better living than he had at the time.

Chuck was out of the house and married by eighteen, but not before learning many of life's lessons. Even though life was difficult, he never forgot the work ethic his mother taught him, a work ethic he has been sure to pass on to his children as well: "I think that's one of the biggest things you can give your child is the knowledge that you got to work for what you want in life." By eighteen, Chuck had already begun to plan for his future and his family's.

The Venturas

Like Chuck and Kathy, Nico and Dalila found in each other a person who understood the other, and, like Chuck and Kathy, Nico and Dalila found common ground through the impoverished childhoods that led both of them to dream of something more. Even though Nico and Dalila did not have to face alcoholism and domestic abuse, the major difference in their dream and that of Chuck and Kathy, which we would call the American Dream, is that Chuck and Kathy's developed within the borders of the United States while Nico and Dalila dreamed of a better life from across the border.

Nico came to the United States thinking it would be easy. He never considered that coming to the United States illegally would brand him a perpetual criminal because this was not the story he or Dalila heard at home as children. Their goal was not to break the law but to achieve a better life. As Dalila put it, "Someone told us we could work here and help our families, and we believed." All they had to do was get the courage to make the arduous journey across the border.

From what Nico could understand from all he had heard in all the stories of people who had gone to America that buzzed about his village, he would be sweeping money from the floor from day one. As a child he was actually told this was a real possibility. Growing up in a rural Mexico, Nico quickly recognized a pattern for success.

He would look around at the village and notice that scattered throughout the shacks were magnificent homes: "I remember just looking around my neighborhood. We had no electricity. We had running water, but no electricity. You could see immediately the people that live there who have very little, but then again in the same neighborhood there's a big house with everything on it—then right in front of it there is just a little house—so you can see the difference." His house was the small domicile, but across the street stood what Nico considered a mansion.

As a small boy, Nico naturally began to wonder how these families seemed to have more money than everyone else. His family worked hard. His father was sometimes gone for months while working at different jobs. His mother left early each morning and came home late from working in the fields nearby. There were even times when she, too, picked up a job far away and left the children at home for extended periods of time during which Nico's sisters assumed their mother's role with the younger siblings.

Despite his parents' hard work, the family was just getting by and often sank into increasing debt. Nico's four older brothers left home to find employment at early ages. In fact, Nico really did not know his brothers very well, but he respected what they did for the family: "They were thirteen, fourteen years old and left the house to start working because my parents couldn't take care of us nine kids. So, I wanted to leave like them to help the family." During our conversation, Nico reminded us frequently that his motivation for leaving was not only his own well-being, but that of his whole family and the family he hoped to have in the future.

What Nico learned was that every family who seemed to find upward financial mobility did so when a family member went to the United States to work. All of his brothers left to find jobs, but none had yet to venture across the border. Therefore, his family had yet to get out of debt. The men who left for the United States, however, sent money back home, and when they returned, their families had already constructed beautiful homes in which their families could live comfortably and debt free for years from the rest of the money made in the U.S. Never did Nico hear of such success going to someone who stayed within the community, even if a family member had left for an education. Upward mobility was always found through moving to the United States. Ultimately, Nico decided to take that chance for his family.

It didn't take long for Nico to convince himself he had to go. Watching his mother and father sacrifice their whole lives to work so that the family could eke by, he knew he had to help: "As a little kid, I always dream of coming to America. I always saw these people coming to America working for a few years then going back to Mexico and having everything, everything I ever wanted, and I saw that they conquered the American Dream. They were able to help their family. That was something that I wanted to do for my family. I wanted to help my mom and my sisters and everybody." Nico explained that in his culture, "We are taught to take care of our own." After doing all he could in Mexico, Nico realized his efforts were not good enough. At a very young age, he began going to the fields to work with his mother, but his added income didn't really make a significant change in the family's life. Comparing the income potential in his hometown to that of his present location, Nico said, "I make more in an hour than they do in a day in Mexico. I make more in one day than they make in a week." This was true not only when he left sixteen years ago, but also today. Finally, he said goodbye and left his family in order to help them.

The year Nico finally decided to leave came when, just

to make ends meet, the family borrowed money. Even with several members of the family working, they were unable to pay all the money back. Nico knew he had to do something, because there was no future in staying. Doing all they could was not good enough, and Nico was growing desperate.

Nico said that some do choose to go to school to better themselves, but this was not an option for him. By going to school, he would have to leave his family without his income for years while he chose the luxury of study. He could not justify this. Besides, he did not have the money to go. Even though he knew his life would be at risk while traversing the desert to cross the border, getting to America was a more attainable dream than earning an education. He felt he had no other options.

When Nico finally told his mother of his plans to leave, she did not forbid him to go, though Nico knew she wanted him to stay. She had always supported her family, but she wrestled with the idea. The rest of the family encouraged her to support Nico, and she did, but even now, she still misses him. She knew she may never see her son again, but she let him go because she knew Nico was leaving to help the family, not to pursue selfish ambitions.

****

Dalila crossed for the same reason Nico did. She was told of unimaginable possibilities in America, and she, too, wanted to make a difference in her family's life. They both knew that crossing the border was dangerous, but they thought the risk would be worthwhile if they could just get to the U.S. Nico's journey took several days. When he finally neared the border, he departed with a group for a twenty-seven hour walk through the desert. They had only a little water and no food. Everyone in his group made it, but they encountered several people who had been left for dead by other groups because they could not keep pace. Nico couldn't rescue them because if he had stopped, he, too, would have

61

been left behind. Looking back, Nico is simply thankful to be alive.

There was one in Dalila's group who was not so fortunate. At a point in their journey, her group was instructed to hide. They heard cars and feared they might be from border patrol. An eight-year-old child in the group panicked. Because he did not know what to do when the group was told to hide, he jumped into the river nearby. The river was moving faster than the boy realized, and he was swept away. Dalila remembers hearing the splash and turning to see the child's red jacket as he was swept underneath the water and carried away. Dalila was seventeen at the time.

Dalila says that if she ever goes back to Mexico, she will never return to the U.S. in this way because the experience was simply too traumatic. Nico agrees. Now, when they speak to family back in Mexico, they urge all of them to stay. There is really no way to understand just how hard it is until on the journey, and for some, it is too late.

Family Dreams

While the biggest difference between the Padgetts' and the Venturas' childhoods was geographic, the trajectory of their lives, while they had the same dream, could not be more different.

The Padgetts

Chuck and Kathy met in high school. They were not supposed to date because, as Kathy put it, "My brother did not like him at all. We were not supposed to go out with each other, because he was a redneck. My brother wanted better for me. He wanted me to get out of what we were in, and he wanted me to move up." What her brother could not see at the time was that although Chuck came from a rough background, he also wanted more out of life. Kathy saw this in Chuck, and their common desire for a good life with safety and stability knit their hearts together.

Kathy did not date often because of her brother, with whom she spent all her time. They were always together. Some boys were too intimidated, while others who did not know them assumed they were dating. This was fine with Kathy's brother, who was very protective of his sister.

Chuck, who had different ideas, was very subtle in his approach. He started tossing M&Ms at her over a wall at school. Once he got her attention out of her brother's sight, he quietly and persistently convinced her to go out with him. They did not have a long courtship. After six months of dating they were engaged, and two months later, they were married. Because they were so young, no one really approved, not Kathy's brother, and especially not Kathy's high school.

After Kathy missed class one day, her teacher began scolding her and asking her where her excuse was. Kathy was on her own now. Her mother and father were no longer responsible for writing an excuse. Kathy finally replied that her husband could write her excuse note if the teacher needed one so badly. The teacher was not amused.

Kathy had assumed that getting married was going to put her on track to become like the television family she had always admired, but after two months of marriage, Chuck and Kathy separated. Married life was not what they had imagined. Ultimately, they reconciled after making a decision many young people never have the maturity to consider. As Kathy put it, they realized that life was "going to be hard with or without each other, so we might as well learn to make it work." Their marriage has grown, though not without rough patches, ever since. They both knew that whatever it took, they were going to make a life together, a life their future children could be proud of, and so they did.

****

Chuck wanted to build his own business and be self-employed. Because he knew it would take hard work to get there, Chuck began to pursue his goal at a very early age. As soon as Chuck became a teenager, he began working with his mother at a Waffle House. At thirteen years old he mopped floors, and, from there, moved up to become a cook. At fifteen, he got a job with a stucco company and learned a trade at which he felt he could excel. His boss was an expert, and Chuck, wanting to learn all he could, became a good apprentice and a fast learner.

When Chuck and Kathy married, he was learning his craft and making his way toward becoming an expert himself. One day, after he had worked in stucco for many years, Chuck promised to help his wife's uncle with a small job underpinning a trailer. Chuck's boss found out Chuck was doing work on the side, confronted him, and gave him an ultimatum: either quit working at his second job with the understanding that from then on, all extra jobs were off limits, or quit working for the stucco crew.

Chuck was a man of his word, and he had promised his wife's uncle he would do the job. He quit his job with the stucco company, but not before learning the trade inside and out. Once he finished the underpinning work, Chuck decided to see if he could pick up odd jobs doing stucco on his own and found work right away. At first his work entailed doing one house here and there, but after proving his ability, Chuck began to build his own company from scratch and found a few guys to help.

An older gentleman who ran his own construction business gave Chuck some start up money and a truck. He also helped Chuck find steady jobs until Chuck could establish a steady flow and make a name for himself. The benefactor's wife even helped Chuck do his book keeping. Once he was confident that Chuck was ready, Chuck's friend sent Chuck out own his own. Meeting in his backyard with his crew, Chuck saw his fledgling business take flight.

The first few years of self-employment did not go well. While he was good at his job and able to find ample work, Chuck's personal life was not as steady. Preferring to leave that time of his life in the past, Chuck didn't go into great detail. He did tell us, however, that he got involved in drug and alcohol abuse: "This is actually right before I got saved. We moved to Tennessee for two years. Had to get my life straight. Wasn't living right. Wasn't doing right."

Chuck found a job with a construction crew in Tennessee, and he and Kathy lived on his hourly wages. They spent a couple of years subsisting, but each day they lived paycheck to paycheck was a day they wasted in pursuing the life they wanted. Chuck knew he could do better back home in Georgia, where he had good business connections and friends who would use his skills. With great determination, he got his life on track, and they went back home. Back home, Chuck was going to rebuild his life, just as he had done before. He was going to work until he had the money to set out on his own.

He quickly found a job with a large lumber company, but after his first day of work, he came home to tell Kathy that it was just not for him. He was tired of working small jobs for others. Kathy was horrified. They had stability and income, but Chuck wanted to throw it all away. Even so, she believed in her husband. He went to work the next day only to tell his employer thanks, but no thanks.

"I turned that down and started doing stucco work again, and picked up some jobs. From there, things progressed" Chuck made this leap of faith at the right time: "It was basically a big boom, whatever you want to call it. The economy just kicked off. There was a lot of construction here, and I got in with some good contractors and started doing all their regular work, and then picking up more contractors from there. Over the first couple of years, I went from three to four guys to—I probably had ten guys to fifteen guys meeting in my backyard every morning, ready to go to work, separating jobs."

Chuck regained his backyard company, but he had no idea it was about to explode. Eventually, Chuck went from providing the physical labor to opening his own stucco supply company. Kathy quit her job and with their daughter, they began to run the office, and the money started coming in.

Although the Padgetts made it clear that achieving their dreams was anything but quick and easy, the time between having a small crew meet in their backyard to the time they had over one hundred employees who worked the entire Georgia coastline seemed to be a blur. They had to work for every penny they earned, but once they made a name for their business, the work itself was never in short supply. The only limitation was their capacity. To compensate, they worked early morning and late nights, often staying at the office or looking over blue prints at home into the early hours of the morning, only to leave a few hours later to do it all again.

Still, work and the money it produced were a means to an end, and that end was a stable, comfortable home for the whole family. With all the work that was pouring in, their dreams of owning a fine home became a reality: "We ended up getting our dream home, close to seven thousand square feet," Kathy told us. "There was four bedrooms, four bathrooms, two half baths, a game room, a sitting room off from our bedroom, my own closet, an office space, hunting room, swimming pool, a barn with a horse, and a pond. Basically everything we had ever imagined or dreamed that we could ever have. We had it." At the height of its success, the business was turning five million dollars per year in stucco and labor.

For twenty-eight years, Chuck and Kathy invested everything in the American Dream and worked to give to their children what they had missed: "We worked very hard to achieve the American Dream, and for a while we had the American Dream. We lived a life that we wanted to live," Chuck told us. Soon, however, the circumstances that made all this possible crashed around them; the American Dream would prove more fragile than the Padgetts could have imagined, and they would have to watch as everything they had worked so hard for slipped through their fingers.

Two strangers from the same country came to the United States at different times, against all odds, each all alone. Both came to make a life for themselves and for their families, and on this journey they found each other. Nico and Dalila, who are from different areas of Mexico, met once they were both in the United States. Nico made his crossing into the U.S. sixteen years ago while Dalila made hers fifteen years ago. Soon after Dalila came into the country, the two met at church. Nico was attracted to Dalila right away. He wanted to take her out on a date, but he did not have a car. He still made the best out of their running into each other at church. Nico knew if she could only get to know him, she would like what she saw: "When I knew she was the one, I did everything I could to show her who I was. I wasn't trying to be anybody, just being myself," he said. He knew if she could see his heart, she would like what she saw.

It was not love at first sight for Dalila. She saw Nico playing in the church band and thought, "Who is that guy?" She did not notice him because of his suave demeanor or charm, but because he was performing in a church band while wearing a tuxedo. She found him to be, in her words, "really weird. He was really weird" It would not take long, however, for Nico to convince her that they should begin a relationship. Dalila had been living in the United States and visiting the church for three months when her courtship with Nico began, and while it was strange for her to fall in love for the first time and even have her first kiss so far away from her home in Mexico, it still somehow felt right.

"Everything seemed so difficult at the time, but once we found each other, nothing else mattered. We had each other," Nico said. Even so, they did not know how fragile this new life together would be. They never realized when they expanded their family, that a day would come when they would feel at every moment the real threat of being torn apart forever. They were new arrivals who were just beginning to understand what it meant to be undocumented in the U.S, a reality never discussed back home as one success story after the other was impressed upon their childhood imaginations.

****

Nico and Dalila shared with us something that I will never forget. As far as I knew, and as far as I had heard from all the rhetoric surrounding this issue, undocumented immigrants come to this country knowing full well the risks that they are taking, not only with the dangers of crossing over, but also with life as an undocumented worker in general. That was not the case for this couple when they were dating and falling in love: "When I came here," Nico said, "it was very difficult to adapt myself to this country. If I would have known that when you cross the border you're an illegal immigrant, someone bad, I think I would've not done it." I wondered what Nico meant. Of course he knew he had to sneak across the border. Was that not enough to indicate he would be illegal?

"Someone told me that we could work here," Dalila said, "that we could help our family, and we believed. We came here when we were very young, and now it's very difficult to go back to our country." As teenagers in Mexico, the only obstacle they knew of when it came to achieving the American Dream was simply the one-time act of sneaking over. Nico continued, "When you are young, you don't think of all the consequences. I didn't. I came to America thinking it was easy — coming in and just start making money the next day." Nico was convinced that he would spend a few years in the U.S., where money was plentiful, make his fair share, and go home to his family: "I was 18 years old when I came to America," Nico paused for a moment. "I'm 34 now. It wasn't easy."

Through their stories it became obvious that when they left Mexico, neither of them really understood what it meant to be "illegal." No one had ever really told them about that part. They knew getting across the border was going to be hard, though they didn't understand how hard, but they imagined that once they made it across, life would be easy. If crossing over was wrong, they would only do it once and never break the law again. They never imagined that once did so, they would be labeled for life. They had no idea that this act would put them in a perpetual state of unlawfulness. They were wrong on so many levels.

There are many practical matters that never occurred to Nico and Dalila until they arrived. Because they did not speak the language, interviewing for a job proved very difficult. It took Nico a long time to find work. Lacking a car presented another major obstacle. Once they found a job, they had to figure out how to get there. Also, the types of jobs that were obtainable were usually seasonal or temporary. Finding a job, therefore, did not provide any lasting security.

Soon, Nico and Dalila learned that undocumented workers were in danger of being deported, but by this time they had risked their lives to come here, and they did not want to leave empty handed. At seventeen and eighteen years of age, they would have found deportation devastating because of the missed opportunity despite the risk taken to get here, but it would not really have been the end of life as they knew it. To their surprise, they did not have much trouble hiding in the shadows, and they eventually learned how to navigate their new home better and better. Whatever being illegal meant, it did not keep them from obtaining work, finding each other, and building a modest life together.

Once Nico and Dalila had children, Dalila explained, "Everything changes. When there's no kids involved, it doesn't matter if there's a police checkpoint and they get us. But we have kids." When they were both single, having a car was not that much of a worry. They had friends who could take them places, but once they were married, they realized they needed a vehicle so that both of them could be sure to get to work. Keeping a steady job, especially as children began to arrive, was crucial, as it is for any family. Now that they had children, they did not want to go back to Mexico for another reason: Their children belong here. Their dreams are here. They will never be able to have the things they know as attainable today if they move to Mexico.

Nico and Dalila worry constantly about what might happen if they are pulled over and found to be undocumented. Though their children are United States citizens, they have no family here who could take them in and watch over them if their parents are deported. Nico says they never take a single day for granted: "Going out the door, it's a risk that we take every day for driving and not having a license. It's scary every time. It gets scarier every time as we hear of people getting arrested and deported immediately. That's a risk we're taking every day. Every morning when we leave home, once we drop off our kids at school, we tell them that we love them every single day, every single morning, knowing that just going to work we're taking the risk of being arrested. You may not know about it. You may not think about it. You may take it for granted, but we don't. We don't. Our kids know that we love them so we tell them everyday as it was a last day, because it could be."

In the eyes of the law, ignorance is not an excuse. Even when someone breaks a law unintentionally, the law still applies. Nico and Dalila came to this country with little knowledge of what it would mean to come across the border illegally. Still, if they had been caught, they would have been sent back under the law. Now, however, they know the full ramifications of the law. They know that they have to hide. They cannot obtain a driver's license or automobile insurance so that now they have even more difficulties to face as illegal immigrants. Many would say they deserve whatever the law has in store for them. Nico and Dalila would also say they now know what the law could mean, and they have to own that fact. Still, they choose to stay. Why?

****

At a time when there was a lot of pressure in their area to deport undocumented workers, Nico and Dalila discussed going back to Mexico as a family to prevent the possibility of being separated. The children were excited about visiting their family, but they had no idea what life was like there. When Nico and Dalila asked about their dreams, the children never considered Mexico a permanent place for their futures. Their lives are here. Their hearts are here. They did not understand that going to Mexico would not be a vacation but a journey that would irrevocably change their dreams forever because their dreams are simply not possible in Mexico. "Our children are here now," Nico said with tears in his eyes. "What do we do? I mean, what do we do." Nico wasn't referring to the physical alone. He was concerned for the hearts of his children, who love the life they have here.

As far as the Venturas are concerned, there is really no going back now. Nico and Dalila live in limbo. They dream of going back home to see their parents. They have been married for the majority of their time in the United States but have yet to meet each other's parents. Returning, however, requires too much risk. Their children's lives began and belong in the United States. To leave this place behind would be to leave everything their children know. No longer is their only priority their families back in Mexico. Now, they have family here. They send money home, but their hearts are now in the U.S.

Their oldest daughter wants to be a pastry chef. The middle child changes her mind each day, and she can do so because she has the freedom to dream in the United States. The youngest is still in diapers, but he belongs here too. While their children anticipate the future, Nico and Dalila constantly look over their shoulders. "I love this country. I love America. It has been my home for 16 years, but somehow I became a prisoner in my own home," Nico said.

"We know what it is like to live back there," Nico said, and he is not willing to make his children move to a place where they would have to start all over, especially if starting over means going back to a place where his children would face great limitations: "They speak Spanish, but not well enough to go to school there. They know how to speak Spanish. They do not know how to read it well. They do not know how to write it. Their dreams are here in the U.S.A. We move to Mexico? It is not fair to them. It's not fair."

Nico adds, "Here is where they have a better chance at life." Speaking particularly about his youngest, Nico said, "I want—oh, gosh—I want him to have everything. Who wouldn't? Who wouldn't want the best for their kids? I want the best for each of my kids." Nico and Dalila came to pursue the American Dream, but now they only hope to stay together as a family. Their other dreams will have to wait. Ultimately, they hope to be a full-fledged part of a community to which they can freely contribute, but for now, the Venturas must hide.

Justice calls for their departure. We cannot deny this. Can we, however, also empathize with their position? They can go back. Nothing is stopping them except for their concern for their children. If we cannot show mercy for Nico and Dalila, can we at least feel sympathy for their innocent children? Often if a parent is deported, judges will decide (as Nico did) that the children have a better chance in America than in Mexico. Against the parents' wills, children have been placed in foster care and put up for adoption when their parents are deported.[xv]

Nico knows he is not innocent now, but he also knows his children are. Do we demand they go home or show compassion while we try to figure out how we can work to protect our borders and consider the real struggles of those who have made it here because we have not properly executed our laws? Maybe there is no one right option here, but can we at least give Nico and people in his situation a moment to make their case, even while we work to protect our nation from future illegal activity? We may never arrive at the right conclusion if we can't at least talk.

The long road of hope for all...

Earlier we spoke about the influences of prejudice and empathy. In this chapter we explored yet another motivation for human behavior: hope. Hope is an integral part of what helps us to follow our dreams for something better, something more.

For both the Padgetts and the Venturas, their hope of realizing their childhood dreams pushed them to seek the lofty goal of the American Dream, a dream that most Americans have been proud to promote as one of the attributes that makes our nation unique and prosperous. It is no wonder that people within and without our country who are desperately seeking more find themselves drawn toward such a dream.

Dreams, however, can be hampered, not least of all by the decisions we make for others as we shape laws for our nation. For Chuck and Kathy, their dream crumbled when they realized that our government lacks either the means or the desire to enforce laws that ensure a level playing field for all. Ironically, they felt the undocumented workers had more advantages than they. They did everything they could to work within the confines of the law, but the law was, in the end, unable to protect their dream. In fact, regulations and laws, at least in part, drove them out of business because the law forced them to pay higher premiums to conduct business than those who were working outside those regulations.

The same system of laws threatens Nico and Dalila's dreams daily. It was open enough to permit them to enter the country, find jobs, compete in the market, earn money, obtain transportation, and secure the means to build the family and home they had always wanted. Still, their lives are precarious because Nico and Dalila are illegal while their children are not. Nico's dream now is that his children can continue to pursue their goals with an intact family.

Can a calm, compassionate conversation open to the

needs and struggles on both sides of the immigration issue occur? That is up to us. One thing is for sure: We are all susceptible to the dream to strive for more and the instinct to provide more for our families. We cannot really blame others for sharing the same aspirations we have ourselves, nor can we deny others their hope. Popular author and psychologist Dr. Scott Barry Kaufman explains its importance:

> *Why is hope important? Well, life is difficult. There are many obstacles. Having goals is not enough. One has to keep getting closer to those goals, amidst all the inevitable twists and turns of life. Hope allows people to approach problems with a mindset and strategy-set suitable to success, thereby increasing the chances they will actually accomplish their goals.*
>
> *Hope is not just a feel-good emotion, but a dynamic cognitive motivational system... Hope leads to learning goals, which are conducive to growth and improvement. People with learning goals are actively engaged in their learning, constantly planning strategies to meet their goals, and monitoring their progress to stay on track. A bulk of research shows that learning goals are positively related to success across a wide swatch of human life.*
>
> *Those lacking hope, on the other hand, tend to adopt mastery goals. People with mastery goals choose easy tasks that don't offer a challenge or opportunity for growth. When they fail, they quit. People with mastery goals act helpless, and feel a lack of control over their environment. They don't believe in their capacity to obtain the kind of future they want. They have no hope.[xvi]*

For both couples, maintaining the will to go on has often been problematic.

Perhaps it is time for us to consider whether or not we

really want to live in a society that proclaims the brilliance of the American Dream but remains unwilling to examine the system of laws that make this dream harder and harder to achieve or maintain? If we accept the status quo, we become complicit in a system that stifles opportunity for some. If we first admit that we have ignored major gaps in the system, we may be able to eliminate some of the inconsistencies that hurt the families who spoke with us, as well as many others like them. Again, our initiative does not propose a solution or assign blame to either side. Rather, we hope to start a civil conversation. If we begin there, we can, perhaps, find a better path for both sides. If, however, we remain unwilling to sit down with those who represent the other side, little will change.

Chapter Five: "Falling In Love"

Some love stories are more romantic than others. For Drew and Mandy, falling in love was fun and exciting. Much more importantly, it was celebrated. For Megan and Desiree, their love story was not as positive because they knew most of the people in their lives would not celebrate with them.

There is falling in love, and then there is falling down while in love. Relationships are never easy, as Megan and Desiree knew from the beginning. Being in a gay relationship was full of pitfalls, especially since family, friends, and colleagues alike would not understand or offer support. For Drew and Mandy, falling down came a little later in their relationship when unanticipated factors hindered their plans to grow the family of their dreams.

While young adults, Megan and Desiree found the pain of falling over their own obstacles almost too much to bear. Thinking hard about life and its meaning, both even wondered if they should really be a part of this life. While a young married couple, Drew and Mandy felt the pain of loss that, for a time, affected their relationship. Beyond simply fighting for their relationships, all four of them had to fight for their souls. Today, they all have one thing, one love that is bigger than any other love, bigger even than their love for each other, and that is their love for God.

Some may view Drew and Mandy, whose lives celebrate and promote the joys of traditional marriage and traditional faith, as mere religious, hardnosed Christians. Yet, as we will see from their story, Drew and Mandy do not adhere to a traditional ideal because of some obscure, inherited dogma. It was their faith that sustained them in their darkest times. They attribute the life they have now, one that has overcome great heartbreak, to their love for God, a love they perceive as a gift that they should never forsake but continually celebrate. Drew and Mandy feel obligated to share the means to the rich life they could not have achieved without their faith.

Some may see Megan and Desiree as persons who have forsaken the moral lessons taught to them as children, as persons who have abandoned any personal responsibility to live according to a purpose. Megan and Desiree, however, are deeply committed to their faith. As Megan insisted many times, their faith is their first love, and it is this love that provided them and many others in their community the strength not to give up on life or let depression and despair consume them. Like Drew and Mandy, Megan and Desiree not only celebrate their faith, but also feel similarly compelled to share their belief that no one lacks worth because of God's love and that life is worth living because all lives have value.

The Thompsons

As far as most of our subjects' stories are concerned, it is easy to see how their backgrounds relate to the issue they speak about in this book. The Thompson's story, however, has a more subtle tie to their firm but gracious support of traditional marriage. In fact, it may seem somewhat disconnected from the issue at first; however, the role their past had in shaping the values they now espouse will ultimately become evident.

Drew and Mandy, who describe themselves as introverts, live in a home that reflects their personalities. Like their owners, the homes of introverted people do not demand attention. Tucked back in the corner of their neighborhood sits the family's small, grey house, whose exterior is rather plain. Tall pine trees shade the home, and the grass struggles for sunlight. Theirs is a normal home hidden in the recesses of a normal subdivision.

Like the interior of an introvert's life, the home's interior is a vibrant and colorful world. Mandy is an artist, and Drew is happy to live in Mandy's visual world. As a pastor, Drew spends most of his time among books anyway, but he appreciates his wife's artistic expressions. Plants hang in glass jars on the bright green walls. Kitchen drawers and cabinets are sketched with hand drawn patterns and letters detailing the contents of each, and the floors are covered in black and white checkered tile. Their cars sit in the driveway because Mandy has converted the garage into her studio, an organized chaos of paint and canvas.

In the dining area hangs Mandy's largest piece of art for their home, a piece that is oddly familiar yet disorienting at the same time. The piece is composed of many small, rectangular fragments of wood in various sizes to create a disjointed but complete silhouette of a tree. The black tree on a white background, upon further inspection, is not one tree at all but a collection of various sections and several species of trees, all arranged to make one large tree, which Mandy identifies as a portrait of their family and home. The Thompsons' family tree brings together a diverse group of people who have become unified by sharing one life sustained by the same deep roots.

****

Drew, who grew up in Tampa, Florida, had a wonderful family experience, but spirituality and religion were not big parts of that upbringing. One day during high school while Drew sat at the lunch table with a girl on whom he had a crush, a mutual friend approached and asked if they would like to come to a Bible study she was hosting at her house. Drew was not at all interested in Bible study, but because he saw this as an opportunity to spend time with his crush outside of school, he responded, "Yeah, man. I love Bible studies. Let's go." Pretending she liked Bible studies as well, his crush agreed. Drew had been to church sporadically as a child, but this experience presented a bit of culture shock. The Orlando Filipino Baptist Church, which was planting a church in the Tampa area, was sponsoring this event. Of course, when he accepted the invitation, Drew had no idea he would be walking into a new cultural experience.

Though he never mentioned whether or not his plan to meet with his crush away from school paid off, Drew recalled the event fondly. Despite his original motive for participating, he was drawn to the experience, especially after he met a Filipino man named Dennis: "He talked about Jesus as if he knew him. He talked about God as if he was talking about his friend or his family member." Drew did not have a similar relationship with God. In fact, up to this point, he wanted God to stay far away. He was afraid that if God got to know the real Drew, God would not be impressed. This event, however, initiated a long spiritual journey for Drew. He began to wonder if he could have a relationship with God like Dennis had? "Here this guy was, not trying to sell anything, but just telling stories about God as one of the everyday members of his life," Drew recalls.

Drew was not one of those converts who gets a glimpse and then immerses himself in a new life because he is a thinker, a measured man, perhaps even a bit of a skeptic. For years he thought about that experience, and then one day at the University of Georgia, Drew encountered the Christian man who would become a mentor. Like Dennis, the man spoke of God as if God were real. He showed Drew what it meant to be a Christian in the everyday life, in relationships, and in decision-making. He made faith real to Drew. Still, Drew simply wanted grace. He was not looking to change the world. He was a math major planning to earn an advanced degree in his field and go on to teach and do research. According to Drew, God had other plans. Drew got the opportunity to work for a youth ministry on the Georgia coast one summer, which led to a full time job at this same ministry. Drew took this job opportunity as a sign and ditched his original plans to begin a new life in ministry.

****

Growing up in a rural Georgia town not far from the coast, Mandy was reared in a devout Christian home. When a young child, she sat on the back pew at church with her grandmother and learned to draw on the offering envelopes: "I guess this is where art and faith first started coming together for me," she said. As Mandy matured, so did her art, through which she discovered all sorts of creative expression. During her teenage years, music was her focal point. Mandy said it was her creativity that kept her grounded in her faith. Whenever she wanted to express herself, she found her deepest expressions to be spiritual. She could not get away from her faith, not that she wished to do so. This passion led her to perform service for others through musical worship at the same ministry Drew was serving. The ministry held its biggest events during the summer, when it would hire interns to facilitate the large influx of youth. When Mandy joined the staff as an intern, she and Drew were immediately attracted to one another. As Mandy puts it, "It was love at first sight, or, at least really, really like at first sight."

Unfortunately, the ministry had a policy forbidding superiors to date interns. Drew and Mandy grew close over the summer and developed a great friendship, but they respected the boundaries set before them. At the end of the summer, Mandy applied for a full time position at the ministry and got it. The rules of the ministry that applied to subordinates and superiors were no longer applicable. They could date. Drew explained it this way: "Baby, the road is wide open for colleagues." Technically, the intern program was not over until all the other interns departed. As soon as the last group drove away, Drew turned to Mandy and said, "So, what are we doing tonight?" They have been together ever since.

Mandy knew right away Drew was the one. She needed him only to ask the right question so that they could spend the rest of their lives together. While Drew felt the same way, it took him a while to make the move: "I knew I loved her, but I had never been married before. I didn't know how that was supposed to work. I didn't know when you're supposed to know, and I think I was waiting for lightning to fall from the sky or a big sign to appear. It just gradually dawned on me. Obviously this is it."

After Drew finished describing his hesitancy to propose, a typical scene in the Thompson home began to unfold. With cameras rolling and the interview in progress, they began to riff. Mandy kicked it off: "I was ready from the first date. I waited a long time for you buddy."

"It took me a while, but I got there. I got there," Drew replied.

"You did."

"I'm a slow student."

"And I'm patient."

They smiled at each other as if no one else were in the room.

Drew's reluctance was not completely his fault. First, he thought he would have to use all the money he had saved for a ring to buy a new car after he totaled his, but, to his surprise, someone offered him a car for a dollar: "I bought a Lincoln Town Car. It was sky blue. It was about a quarter mile long. It was great."

After dodging that crisis, Drew had to ask Mandy's father for his blessing, "...which was a lot harder than proposing to her. Her dad is tough, but he grudgingly gave me permission to marry his daughter." All that was left was to pop the question, and Drew had a perfect plan. They would spend Christmas apart, Mandy with her parents in Georgia and Drew with his parents in Texas, but after Christmas, Mandy would fly to Texas, where Drew would ask for her hand in marriage the day after she arrived.

Drew's entire family was in town. Drew's brother had brought his fiancée, and Drew's sister had brought her boyfriend. The night Mandy flew in, Drew's sister's boyfriend came running in the house to tell everyone they had great news: He and Drew's sister were engaged. Drew's future brother-in-law had beaten him to the punch. Drew did not want to detract from their happy moment, but he was stuck. He had already asked permission from Mandy's father, bought a ring, and told everyone back home they would return engaged. At this point, Mandy began to feel like a bit of an outsider. Both of Drew's siblings were now engaged. Why was Drew dragging his feet? A little upset with his brother-in-law for "jumping the gun," Drew took all the frustration in stride and went on with his plan. He asked Mandy to take a walk with him, and when they reached a nearby park, Drew proposed to her on the monkey bars. She, of course, said yes. When they returned with their happy news, Drew's father thought they were joking. He couldn't believe all three of his children were engaged at the same time. After he saw they were serious, Drew's father simply said, "Your mother is going to have a heart attack."

And so it happened that all three siblings married in the same year: Drew and Mandy in April, Drew's sister and her fiancé in May, and Drew's brother and his fiancée in December. Drew and Mandy were finally on track to begin a beautiful family, but they found that the beauty they were seeking was unavailable to them as they had imagined. They would have to wrestle with life and faith to find new visions of beauty, the sort of beauty displayed in Mandy's disconcerting yet captivating depiction of the Thompson Family Tree.

The Hodges

She was her parents' little miracle. Ever since these high school sweethearts Eric and Vicky Hodge married they had dreamed of having a big family. They already had two healthy boys, four and six, and Vicky very much wanted her little girl. After the boys were born, the Hodges suffered two miscarriages and worried they wouldn't be able to continue growing the family of their dreams.

Now, they were expecting for their fifth time, and even with the lingering grief and worry of the previous losses, Eric and Vicky held to hope. At first, the pregnancy was normal, but at four months, Vicky started to bleed. The Hodges feared the worst. They were going to lose yet another child. In an effort to save the child, her physician put Vicky on bed rest and prescribed hormones for her.

For the rest of the pregnancy, Vicky, remaining on hormones and bed rest, prayed for a miracle. "Every night when I would go to bed," Vicky said, "I would just thank the Lord that he had given me another day with this baby." At about eight months, when she was feeling fairly confident her child was going to make it, she added a small request to her prayer of thanks: "Lord, if you really wanted to surprise me, it'd be wonderful if it would be a little girl." She had carried the baby ten months when her doctors decided to induce labor.

The doctor had warned Vicky that the hormones she took to save the pregnancy could have an effect on the child, but her fears were soon gone. "I had a wonderful delivery. When she was born, the doctor stuck her right in my face and said, 'She's perfect!'" The relief and joy were overwhelming. The Hodges named their daughter Megan, and took her home to meet the rest of her family. Becoming her daddy's little girl, her mother's closest confidante, and her older brothers' biggest fan, Megan grew up happy with her place in a wonderful home filled with love, faith, and hope. One secret, however, would threaten her relationship with her family.

****

When Megan was ready to leave home to start a life of her own, she wasn't quite sure what that life would look like. Although she had never seriously considered a life in the military before, once Megan began to think about the possibility, she slowly came to think it might be a good fit. She was already accustomed to a transient lifestyle because her father's job had moved the family around during Megan's formative years. "I grew up in Indiana and lived there until I was about nine. We ended up moving. Spent [ages] ten to fourteen in Ohio, then moved to Knoxville, Tennessee. Spent a year there, and then ended up moving from there to Jonesboro, Arkansas. That is where I ended up graduating high school." Megan then moved back to Tennessee to attend Lee University in Cleveland and, eventually, the Church of God seminary on Lee's campus for her first graduate degree.

Moving around so much at a young age had an impact on Megan. She not only got used to it but actually enjoyed it. Now, she told us, every few years she gets the itch to move, to meet new people, to make new friends, to invest in new communities. What other vocation could offer such an opportunity than the military. The only problem was, Megan thought, that her dreams were leading her elsewhere. She was on track to be in ministry, not the military.

Megan was approaching the end of her studies in seminary and needed to decide on her next steps in life. "I remember very distinctly telling my parents, 'I don't know what I want to do,' and they told me, 'Well, you've got to figure it out.'" Megan was torn, because she knew she wanted to be involved in some aspect of Christian ministry; she was just not sure how to narrow her focus. She loved it all, and wanted to do it all: teaching, preaching, and counseling. She was convinced there was no job that could encompass all of her ambitions. Megan felt that though pastors do a bit of it all, they don't have the opportunity to do it all to the degree she desired. Graduation was nearing and Megan was feeling the pressure.

"One of my friends said, 'You know, have you ever thought about being an Army or Navy chaplain?'" Megan responded quickly, "What? No. Why would I think about that? I don't want to go into the Army. I don't want to go into the Navy. I don't want to do any of that stuff. I really don't want to do any of that physical stuff, if I'm being honest.'"

Later that night, Megan, still feeling adrift about her future, decided to humor herself and look into the Army's chaplaincy. When she sat down at her computer and searched for information, she was shocked: "I about fell on the floor, because it said, 'Join the Army chaplaincy, where you can preach, teach, and counsel.'" There it was, everything Megan was looking for. She began to grow excited, but she wasn't sure she could make such a huge step alone.

Continuing her research, Megan discovered that the program had a "buddy system" through which people who enlisted together for chaplaincy would be stationed together. Megan had a friend in seminary she thought might be interested in learning about the chaplaincy program as well. She, like Megan, wanted to participate in all aspects of ministry, and they worked well together on top of that; however, when Megan approached her about joining with her friend, she was a bit shocked by the answer. "She just looked at me and said, 'Meg, shut up.' I was so confused. She was a sweet girl.'" It took Megan a moment to recover, but when she did, Megan, though uncomfortable, continued the conversation, trying to explain herself and discover why her friend had such a visceral reaction. It turned out that Megan's friend was not angered by the suggestion, just very, very surprised.

"Her dad was a Special Forces colonel," Meagan told us, "and, when she first got to seminary, she had been out on a prayer walk, walking and talking to God. She said, 'You know, God, if you sent somebody to come along for me to go to the military with and serve as a chaplain, I would totally do that.' That had been three or four years earlier." So, they joined, and assumed their first church assignment together. The Commanding Officer (CO) in charge of their appointment purposefully gave the two young women a small assignment. Only nine people attended their service.

Megan thinks her CO assumed that two girls, fresh out of their seminary training, would struggle in their first assignment. He couldn't know the extent of Megan's drive and passion, both inspired by her family. Her brothers had always been a success in their careers, and she was not about to let them outshine her. She was going to honor their example by being the best chaplain she could be.

By the end of the assignment, the service had grown so large that her church had to rent a theater on Sundays to accommodate the congregation. Megan knew she was where she was supposed to be, and her CO knew it as well. She fell in love with her job of serving the soldiers, and she climbed the ranks rapidly: "When I finished up my third rotation as a battalion chaplain, I came out on the promotion list and was promoted to Major in 2011 and was placed in an assignment that I didn't even realize was an issue. They had never put a female brigade chaplain in a brigade combat team slot." It was a two-year assignment that proved to be incredibly difficult, but Megan was not one to avoid a challenge. Again, she excelled. Throughout her career, Megan presided over large congregations and helped to carry many burdens of soldiers struggling with life.

She was a chaplain, and she was good at it, but she was holding something about herself back, something deeply rooted that wouldn't go away no matter how hard she tried to deny its existence. She felt it was a threat to everything she had worked so hard to build. She was helping so many people, but when she met with other soldiers who shared her hidden feelings, she confronted a crisis. Would she come out of the shadows to "be real" and "authentic" with others in the same situation, or would she continue to hide for the sake of her position?

****

For Megan, moving around a lot encouraged her to be outgoing, but for Desiree, moving around as a child meant quite the opposite. Transience hindered her from making many significant connections. Her upbringing was different too. Her mother and father never married. When Desiree was very young, her mother married another man, who adopted Desiree. Her new father was in the service, and once she joined his family, Desiree found herself moving around more times than she could remember. Unfortunately, the marriage did not last. At the age of ten, Desiree watched as her parents parted ways. Instead of staying with her biological mother, who was the anchor in her chaotic life, Desiree stayed with her adoptive father. Continuing to move from place to place, Desiree had a hard time making friends. Changing schools often, sometimes in the middle of the school year, made making friends even more difficult for the shy young girl.

When I asked Desiree about missing out on a normal childhood, she gently corrected me. She explained that in her experience, there were many children in the exact same situation. In fact, most of the people she grew up with and now oversees as a Warrant Officer for the United States Army come from a similar background. Desiree does not feel sorry for herself because of her past. She put her head down and did what she had to do to succeed. She now oversees a crew that works on weapons systems, and though she is proud of her service, she is not one to brag.

Here is Megan's take on Desiree: "She is so not a showman, but if anybody could brag, it should be her. She doesn't. She constantly gives, gives to homeless, gives to the soldiers under her. It's just a daily part of her. You are not going to get an exuberant, extroverted love out of her, but you are going to get the stuff that matters. Just investment and care. She is a big sister and role model for her soldiers. You can hear it in the way they text her, the way they call her, the way they rely on her when they are in need. She makes sure those who are at their lowest know, "You are important. You matter." You just don't see that a lot. People often want to know what can you give me, but not what can I give to you." Megan was not speaking simply in general terms, although this is true enough, but she was speaking of Desiree as a CO. Most officers want to get much out of those under them, and Desiree does as well, but she does this by giving herself to them, even if this means caring for them deeply.

As an adult, Desiree retains her shy personality, a trait that makes it hard to be vulnerable, and nothing makes one more vulnerable than trying to connect with others in their struggle, yet this is her life. Sharing a word of encouragement that comes from deep within can be almost physically painful for introverts, but when Desiree sees a need, she feels compelled to help.

Like Megan, Desiree knew something about her life was different. She was not what she had expected to be. She was not sure at first what her feelings were, and at the age of ten, she often tried to pray her feelings away, but, like Megan's, they did not leave. She was a confidante for so many others, but with these feelings she often struggled alone. She even accepted being solitary as her lot in life. "Before I met her," Desiree said of Megan, "I truly thought that being gay meant I would be alone. I really thought that that's just the way it's going to be: me, my mom, my brother and eventually just me and my mom living the rest of our lives out that way."

Desiree knew her mother had constantly struggled to keep their family together. This is why she had to live, for a time, without her. Early in Desiree's career, she decided to bring her mother and brother into her home to support them. This was it for her. Her life as a gay person who did not really belong to anyone else was sealed, she believed, and now that she had made the decision to care for her mother and brother, a commitment she was going to honor for the rest of her life, she stopped imagining she could find someone who would not only accept her for who she was, but also accept her family's presence in her life and home.

At the heart of the issue was faith, the same faith to which Megan had dedicated her vocational life. There were times when both Megan and Desiree would hear from others who were unaware of the women's orientation that people like them were not welcome. Megan and Desiree both served the military for a while before finding someone to confide in, someone who would say, "You still belong."

Section III: Horizons

The burden of listening

Right or wrong, miraculous or haunting, every person's story leads to an outcome. While we can overcome our pasts, as our subjects were able to do so to various degrees, one truth remains: Our past has a bearing on our present. This is true for our individual, family, and even cultural histories. Everyone's formative years are full of incidents and influences that affect the trajectory of his or her life. Of course, we remain culpable for our actions, but the manner in which our lives unfold is affected by more than our conscious choices. Our backgrounds contribute as well. We must, therefore, work together, despite our disagreements, to move forward. This means that we must become listeners and students of people's individual and cultural pasts.

Often we would like to believe that we are self-made men and women and to think that all we have and believe about the right way to live has all been earned by pulling ourselves up by our bootstraps and making an honest, diligent attempt to discover the right path. Those of us who consider ourselves a success, however, owe a great deal to our communities, families, and those far in the past who paved the path we now walk. In turn, we will continue to shape that path, not only for ourselves, but for our children and culture as well.

While it might be gratifying to take full credit for our accomplishments in life, we would be more than a little prideful not to give thanks where it is due. We reflect on the courageous acts of men and women in our past. We look to America's Founding Fathers and credit them the success of a great nation, a success that we believe has paved a path for us to be personally successful as well. We memorialize events such as Independence Day and commemorate those who sacrificed so much to fight for good during World War II. While many of us see the need to give thanks for such events, we still look at the successes and failures of others as if those triumphs and defeats rest solely on their shoulders as individuals. If we are going to be a people who celebrate the past, we must respect it enough to acknowledge that it also has the potential to influence the future negatively as well.

The past cannot work as a catalyst for future possibilities when we only romanticize it. The past can also produce failures that lead to impossibilities, or, at the very least, improbabilities. If those among us who are successful attribute at least some of our success to others who have helped us in the past, why do we refuse to acknowledge the past's effect on those who struggle, even those who have made poor choices? Did they blaze that trail all on their own, or did they follow a path well worn?

There is room to celebrate and lament our past, which can function as a hand up or a push down. With this in mind, we must realize that our own future, the future of our children, and the future of our nation now depend upon how we live in the present. As Vernon lamented in our *Introduction*, the atrocities of stealing Native Americans' land and building wealth through slavery still have an impact on our culture today and on those whose families were in the direct wake of those atrocities. Vernon was also correct when he expressed in the *Introduction* that while we have the chance to pave a better way forward, we cannot do so and continue to incite cultural war over cultural healing because doing so will doom the future to perpetuate past hardships and shift the burden of reconciliation to our children and grandchildren and beyond. We have a past we can build upon and can repent of. May we be the generation to recognize that individual and cultural paths shape the future and to work together to boost both the individuals around us and the culture as a whole.

****

As a black father to black children, Vernon strongly advocates that young lives are shaped by more than choosing right or wrong. Children are subject to all the cultural messages that tell them who they are. Vernon explained his premise this way:

"I think the battle of image is huge. It's bad enough that we've had an image problem with black America because we have dealt with many issues improperly, but then to have those imposed on us and expected of us by society in general, it's a huge, huge challenge that has to be dealt with. If you don't see yourself as successful, if you don't see the potential that you can succeed, then a lot of us make the best of failure.

Those that are in the drug world and selling drugs, if that's all they can do, if their image is to be successful and to be great at what they do and that greatness happens to be selling drugs, then they're going to have the rings. They're going to have the car. They're going to have the life — the guns and the weapons, and the look, and the cut, and the whole process that goes along with being successful in that world. They'll be good at being bad. So many of us, when we try to convert a bad kid into a good one, say, 'If you could just take that power and turn it into something good, if you could just take all of that thought process that you put into selling drugs and become a real pharmacist you could cure cancer.'"

"'But they — they'd never let me cure cancer. But I could make a mean fix and make you think you don't have cancer.' So, they become good at their role, at the image, the failed image that has been presented, and they have swallowed that pill and made the best of that pill so we have thuggery now at a level we didn't have before because the options exist. The options do not exist for them to see themselves as successful.

"'Do you see that you can get a job, and that you can fight the good fight? And have a good career? And make $100,000 dollars?'

"'No. But I can make $100,000 a month selling drugs.'

"And that's success. It's not good success. It's not right success. But it is a level of success."

Again, our words shape us, not just in the name-calling and slander, but in the overall perceptions and stories we tell about ourselves and others. The entertainment industry continually portrays young blacks as drug dealers and those parts are often the only ones available. We often hear the term *thug* tossed about in reference to a young, black man who makes a bad decision. Ultimately, young black men themselves may own that stereotype and come to believe that the picture they've been presented is also the expectation of society. Of course, this influence is applicable not only to the black community but to all communities. We must, therefore, learn to celebrate the best in each other and determine not to focus only on the worst. When we speak in negative terms about each other, often our words lead to self-fulfilling prophesies, if only because we limit what the other can do in our own minds.

When we believe whole groups of people amount only to their stereotypes, it is no wonder many from these groups have difficulty finding a job because they are not trusted. Different expectations and treatment can begin earlier in life with those who shape children for the future. Teachers, for example, may grow frustrated with children whose difficult backgrounds have a negative impact upon the children's behavior and performance at school. Could it be that in their frustration they subconsciously choose not to spend as much time on the ones they believe will not amount to much anyhow? Our words shape our stories, and our stories shape our perceptions, which we often find hard to move beyond. The past, then, can inhibit our ability to appreciate the possibilities of helping the groups we have already pigeonholed find a future.

We have to find a way to move beyond what others say of us. That healing process begins when we are ready to repent for our part, whether intentional or not, in perpetuating damaging stereotypes. The process further depends upon our ability to put behind us what others say. As Vernon said, "You have to forgive the people that taught you that, and you have to forgive yourself for believing them." The anger those who have been harmed by stereotypes experience is certainly understandable, but it must eventually give way to forgiveness if we are to move toward healing.

A new perspective on sharing our opinions

What each of us expects of the future is defined by where we stand in the present. Some of us have a better vantage point than others. For all of our subjects, life's circumstances have led them to their present position, and these experiences, in part, have molded how they see the world now, and given shape to how they imagine their futures.

Hopefully, when we hear others speaking of their pasts, we will desire to breathe life into their futures through offering advice, but this is not enough. As Vernon's illustration of an impressionable child turned drug dealer shows, we are not going to have a meaningful conversation until we know why others think as they do. Even when we think the other is in the wrong, we will not be able to address the wrong by simply attacking the other. We have to get to the root of the issue. There we will find one of two things: a deeper pain that remains unaddressed or a faulty perspective on our part.

Because we all have a past, we have experiences and lessons we may wish to share with others, especially those in whom we anticipate needless mistakes. In order to be constructive and build trust, however, we must also be willing to hear not only the others' position, but also the stories that got them to where they are today. We owe others their dignity, which we may best discover the resources to afford them when we attempt to place ourselves in their shoes. The conclusions we draw about our own lives may be accurate, and our views about the way we should live may reflect wisdom we have acquired through our successes and failures. It is certain that many who have very similar experiences come to very different conclusions, some good and some less so.

Nonetheless, as Vernon pointed out, we cannot help others see a different angle if we do not take the time to learn about the direction from which theirs comes. People can be very wrong because they are very hurt. We have a responsibility to validate their pain and refrain from offering advice if, in fact, we are merely criticizing instead of extending empathy. Do most of us not have people in our lives who took the time to listen first so that they could then share a new perspective that changed our lives?

To further Vernon's illustration, we might imagine what many of us would wish to say if we had the opportunity to speak to an incarcerated drug dealer: Our knee-jerk response would be,"Grow up and get a job!" or "Hey, you can have a good life, a stable family, and a good job. Just look at me."

What is so wrong with that? Such statements ignore our pasts. Those of us who experienced stable homes and attended good schools cannot deny a strong advantage others lack simply because they were born into different circumstances they did not choose. We cannot deny that social and business connections can also provide some of us a boost in acquiring scholarships and job opportunities we may not otherwise merit. Of course, the American Dream suggests that one can come from nothing but rise to greatness, and we could all provide examples of this construct. Many of us who scratch our heads at someone else's lack of success, however, did not make it on our own. Rather, we benefitted from predecessors who overcame humble circumstances so that our advice about pulling themselves up by their bootstraps to those who had no one to pave the way and make success easier to achieve is hollow. There is no one-size-fits-all answer to the real problems that hamper segments of our society.

The problem with listening to others and affording everyone a voice is the vulnerability we must be willing to embrace in order to do so. We also have to be patient when we want to become defensive. If we first know where others stand and how they came to adopt that stance, we can avoid the frequent mistake of simply talking past each other. Ultimately, we may find more common ground than we had expected.

****

What is it we dread in coming to know people right where they are? What is it we imagine will go wrong if we allow them to state their case, even if that case contradicts our ways of thinking? Do we shut others down because we fear their opinions, if heard, might diminish ours, convince us we are wrong, and challenge our standards? Perhaps we are afraid our emotions might somehow betray us. Certainly, risk is involved, but many worthwhile things entail danger. A conversation in which we listen as avidly as we speak and keep our negative emotions at bay need not threaten us. If we are willing to befriend someone with or from whom we differ, we don't have to respond to their views immediately. We can reasonably say, "I am not sure what to say right now, but I want to think about this and talk with you again." If our standards are still fragile after this, they may want reexamination.

In this section we will look closely at how life's struggles have led to new futures for each of our subjects. As Vernon illustrated with his explanation of why some children grow up to become drug dealers, that which is most telling may be the human spirit's desire to make a way in any situation, no matter how difficult.

Our subjects, who speak from opposite sides of the issues we are examining, have presented their pasts to show how the past shaped their futures. We may already wish to validate one perspective and debate another, but we must continue to listen intently until the end, for only then can we justifiably claim to understand. In the meantime we must extend the same grace we would wish for ourselves in telling our own stories.

****

Fortunately, none of our subjects, even though they have all faced difficult life circumstances, chose such a negative course such as the one Vernon presented, yet our point remains: We must allow the other to be heard so that we all might come to identify what it is we would truly want to say, once we understand, and, perhaps, allow us to see our own blind spots and prejudices against the other.

Of course, we each enjoy the right to choose our own paths, but we have to do so within a society of which we are a part and to which we bear a responsibility. Wouldn't it be better to foster through patience and compassion a way to share our differences so that we all might grow in grace and understanding? We will not always get what we want when we work this way. The process will undoubtedly move slowly and require much labor, but nothing worth having comes easily. Ultimately, we can create something lasting as people who disagree but fundamentally want the same things: a home and an egalitarian nation that will stand for the sake of future generations.

If we come to see this human desire to make something of our individual situations as a need we all share, perhaps we could, instead of seeking only our individual desires, foster growth and make something of the world together because, like it or not, we all will strive to make something. We certainly owe it to each other to try. As Vernon put it from his own experience in influencing young lives, "When we fight and we tell our kids to choose this way and not that way, our reasons for telling our children to cut their path the right way have to be as strong and morally balanced against the forces that tell a kid otherwise. That cuts across race too."

It cuts across race. It cuts across cultures. It cuts across beliefs. We all live inside an identity and societal expectations; therefore, as members of society, we need to speak life and not prejudice into each other's lives, and someone has to go first, even at the risk of rejection. To end the frustrating gridlock that permeates both our political system and our culture, we must be willing to take this long, arduous road with others, to look across the aisle and offer a hand, not a fist. We have to fight for and not against each other lest we see our prejudices fulfilled in the other because we were not willing to combat the apathy and let others fall.

When Vernon reflected upon the lies that many young people of his own community have accepted because society expects them to behave at particular levels, he implored, "The history of blacks cannot be repeated on the other fronts that exist in America today." We must be unwilling to consign a person or group to fulfill our own expectations. We must resist the urge to tell them just where they will end up, and, instead, be willing to walk together.

For the Jacksons, encountering children who have a hard road ahead is a daily journey. We all know the statistics pertaining to children who come from unstable homes and face harsh futures, but the Jacksons have seen real hope engendered in others because they were willing to listen and help pave a new path while understanding the hardships of the past. They are a symbol of what it can mean if people will listen.

Chapter Six: "Fostering Redemption"

A small moment in time

Portia told us of one of their more difficult situations as a foster family: "We had a young girl come into our lives whose mother was on crack cocaine and meth, and she left her with us at night. One time she came back and said that she was just not going to come back anymore. She couldn't afford the child and asked if we would keep her. We told her we would." The Jacksons, suddenly put in a difficult position, decided to become this child's permanent family, but the emotional roller coaster was not over.

Portia continued the story: "[The mother] decided that after a while, she wanted the child back. So, she came back and got the child and moved." Portia told us it was very hard on them. They had become emotionally attached to the young girl and believed her biological mother was making a poor decision, because the mother had not yet gotten her life on track. "We asked her to leave the child with us until she got herself clean. She said she couldn't live without her child." And that was that. She had the rights to the child, and they vanished from the Jackson's lives.

Eight years passed before they heard anything else from their foster daughter. Now a teenager, she called to report that she had experienced a horrible life. She wanted to know why Portia and Vernon had not kept her, had not fought for her. Portia explained to her that they had, but "that was your mom. She gave birth to you. She had all the rights." It turns out, Portia told us, that the mother did get clean, but somehow, in the process of taking care of herself, she lost sight of her child's needs. "She kind of abandoned the child," Portia said. Despite all of this, the young girl had more to report, a silver lining. She had fought for herself. She said that life had been hard, in fact, something of a horror, but overall, she still found her way. Portia told us that when the girl, called she said, "I was able to make it. I thought about the things you guys told me, that you guys instilled upon me. I just want you to know that you are my parents."

Those words carried such a powerful emotional impact. A child who had lived only a fraction of her life under their roof still thought of the Jacksons as her parents. She had filtered everything she endured through her experience with the Jacksons, and she attributed her positive decisions, which made a miserable life bearable and even possible to overcome, to this husband and wife she still considered her parents.

Portia told us that this conversation changed their lives. She knew she didn't have the power to change the circumstances that hurt all of them, but she had never really considered what a deep impact such a small amount of time would have upon a child. Despite the child's feelings of rejection and confusion about why the Jacksons did not keep her, their efforts on her behalf still made all the difference.

The potential for what foster parenting could do for children became manifest for the Jacksons. Portia continued, "Everybody needs to have a chance at life." For Portia, this means everyone needs at least one thing: "Everybody needs to get a good foundation when they are young so that they can weather whatever life throws at them." The Jacksons might not be able to stay with their foster children the whole way, but they can give them something to stand on and believe in.

Fostering for a future

It is a noble thing to adopt, and Portia already knew this from being raised by a mother who was always willing to make more room. Adoption is hard work. It can cost parents a lot of sleep while they wrestle with the adoption process and a lot of grief when they reveal to the child his or her adoption. It also demands a financial sacrifice, yet as most adoptive parents would surely attest, the chance to share the love of their home with a child who would otherwise go without is a blessing that far eclipses any costs. Parenting a child is always a gift.

To many people, fostering and adopting are somewhat synonymous terms, or, at least, very similar because they have never really interacted with the culture of adoption and fostering. While the two systems are complex and interrelated, broadly speaking, they differ in their aim. Adoption is the process of legally and permanently including an outside person into an existing family unit. Fostering is the process of taking care of a child for a time during which the child's parents or guardians have lost the means to provide but are in the process of attempting to regain means of care. While foster care can lead to a permanent adoption, the common hope of the foster system is that the child in foster care can eventually leave the care of the foster family and return to the original family, normally biological, after that family has had time to get back on its feet.

Fostering comes with it own unique set of challenges. Because children often arrive from highly stressful situations, they are not always capable of responding with the sort of compliance parents normally expect from children. These children often have various medical and psychological needs, and sometimes they can pose a risk for other children in the home. Perhaps the toughest aspect of all, however, is the willingness to form a bond with them even though they will eventually move on and hopefully return to their families. Most of us will never know what it is like to invest in the life of a child as if we were the parents but lack the privilege of finishing the job. The Jacksons have faced this challenge, not just once, but time and again. Currently, they are caring for three very young girls.

"I worked for the Department of Family and Children Services," Portia told us. "In this area, there weren't enough foster homes." What Portia observed was that many of the foster homes her particular branch of DFCS had to use were outside their county, and this made the process of fostering very difficult. Parents who wanted to visit their children while they worked to be reunified often could not because transportation and the costs included were not available to them for such distances. This put tremendous stress on all parties involved: Portia's department, the parents of the children they served, and the foster parents who had to care for children who could not understand why they could not visit their moms and dads. Because there were 150 children in foster care and only 50 homes in the area, Portia told her husband she could not sit by while family after family lost contact with the children.

Vernon admitted that, at one point, when they already had four children in the home, he felt they had as much as they could handle, but he remembered his wife's dream and then had one of his own. Vernon wiped his eyes yet again and began to tell us of his dream with a shaky voice: "It was a spiritual revelation of children falling and hitting the ground, and nobody caught them. They would just fall." Vernon felt this deep sense that someone was supposed to catch these children, but when he looked around in panic, he could not see who was letting the children fall. Then, he realized what the dream meant. When he looked down, he saw that his hands were empty, ready to catch: "My hands were the ones that were supposed to catch these children, but they were distracted." That is when, Vernon told us, his wife's dream and the ministry of care within the Jackson family was finally etched as an indelible mark into his spirit. Before that, he had appreciated what they did for others, but now it was a part of him, a mark on his soul.

While Vernon recounted the many experiences they have had as foster parents, it was obvious to our team just how difficult it must be to care for those who have never experienced care, but Vernon's tireless optimism shifted the burden into an opportunity. He found a way to be positive though these children often come with little or no experience with parental guidance: "One or two percent of what we do for our own kids is more than these kids will ever have. So, we are in a place where we have some extra love in our hearts. We had some parenting leftover." Vernon tells us this love has expanded as, one by one, his biological children have grown up and left the home. "Other kids don't replace your birth children, but they allow you to do something with all that heart and all those emotions and all that love you have for children. They respond to it so well." The Jacksons see parenting their own children not as a task to complete, but as an opportunity to hone the lifelong skill of caring for others. And what is the end result of using this skill for the sake of foster children? Vernon tells us, "The children transform, having their needs met. They begin to believe in life again. They begin to love again, and they begin to respond."

The Jacksons told us that the transformation love brings is never less than miraculous. They spoke of what it is like when older children come into the home. Often, they are the most frustrated and the least trusting. They have, in many ways, been broken, and it is the Jackson family's calling to mend those wounds. The older kids are often full of fear of not getting a meal, so they hoard food. They fear being harassed when they do something as simple as using to the bathroom. Over time, however, they relax. They learn that the food is always there and won't be limited. Having privacy is never questioned. Being able to feel safe is a possibility. The Jacksons are happy to provide those small revelations that love does really exist.

Vernon told us he had learned some things from foster care he could have never learned from simply raising his own children. Vernon and Portia learned first hand that love is truly limitless, and it is a strong enough force to help one carry on in the most difficult circumstances. Even when children come into the home angry, unresponsive, and perhaps somewhat destructive, love is a medicine that heals both the child and the tired, broken state of the foster parents, who tirelessly serve: "It is a fuel to go a thousand miles through another round of trouble to try and stop another one from hitting the ground," Vernon says.

The second thing the Jackson's learned was that hate destroys. The worst part of hate is that it is self-destructive. Love is limitless, but hates limits, and the only hope for destructive hate is love. While the Jackson's value getting children when they are in the most formative years, even older children can learn. We can all learn from someone willing to love us.

Sowing and Reaping

Vernon and Portia are firm believers that love is inborn and hate is taught. In the *Introduction* I argued that prejudice is, in part, a byproduct of human nature. We are wired to make assumptions, but those assumptions, the Jacksons attest, are based on a multitude of small observations children make when they watch adults interact with the world, and while adults might be cautious enough to guard some of their deepest assumptions during these interactions, children are perceptive enough to perceive the smallest clues. Unlike adults, however, children are not always adept at hiding how they think and feel. If they are not allowed to love others and see real love displayed toward others, especially those who are different, by their own communities, they will learn to hate.

Constantly, Vernon told us children do not care about race. They may wonder why someone does not look like them, but theirs is an innocent curiosity. When a child lashes out at a person of another color with racial slurs, the child has learned that behavior and terminology someplace.

What the Jacksons experienced with one of the foster children still troubles Vernon today, not because of what the child did, but because such behavior had to have come from somewhere else. "We've had all kinds of children, but one of the white kids that we had came from a home that was not racially balanced." While in the Jacksons' care, the little girl had called her bus driver a nigger, "and she also came back and hugged us. So, she didn't understand." Vernon told us that the girl was simply unaware of how to navigate dealing with people who were different from her, and it was now their job to teach her this new lesson, to contradict the lies she had learned, and to help her transition to a place where she could really feel remorse for those sorts of feelings: "It was interesting when she learned that the people that cared for her the most and had the greatest impact on her life did not look like her," Vernon explained.

The impact of the lessons the Jacksons taught would not end there. The love continued to spread. The Jacksons were committed not only to giving the child a good foundation, but also to reconciling her to her family, the family from whom she had learned to associate hurtful racial slurs with people like Vernon and Portia. "They got a chance to meet us and redefine their image of what black people are and do and how they express themselves," Portia said. While the family watched the obvious healing their little girl experienced in the Jackson home, their own process of racial healing began.

Vernon pointed out a fundamental lesson about suffering. The child obviously had deep-seated pain. A little girl does not call her bus driver such a name unless there is something wrong. What we have to learn from this is that when we are in pain, we are often incapable of locating the problem; instead, we simply shift it to something we do not understand. Vernon continued, "Everyone can contribute to how well this country works if they're taught you don't have to hate what you are not. You don't have to despise what you are not. In fact, you can love what you are not, and then that frees you to even love yourself more." When we refuse to hold on to hate, we can enjoy our lives so much more than we can if we are forever bitter. Change often happens one person at a time. This child would never have had the chance to grow if the Jacksons had not been willing to foster her by sharing all the benefits of family while never expecting her to give them anything in return.

We constantly encounter people who have scars that

love can begin to heal. Vernon and Portia do not believe in better as an ideal. They know better is a viable option because they have given a piece of themselves to each of these children. "We are able to give them a destiny, not fitting of their beginning, but in what God has for them," Vernon said. For Vernon and Portia, the dream of seeing a nation heal through the willingness of some to become vulnerable to others not like them is possible. It is a reality they experience every day, but it does not begin with a vote or a program we install on a national level. It begins with someone who is willing to love another right where he or she is. The Jacksons do not suggest we give another who is not like us a place in our hearts because it sounds ideal, but because they have seen healing, true healing, in practice.

We must remember with the Jacksons that hate destroys. When we encounter hate, we can bring healing with love. We never know what leads a person to hate. We can only be vulnerable in the hope our compassion might reveal another way to live. Will it always work? No. There are times we must eventually walk away, but giving love a chance to overcome is always worth a shot.

Chapter Seven: "New Communities"

Chuck and Nico both had to reevaluate their dreams. Life did not go as they had imagined, and after they accepted their circumstances, they had to move forward for the sake of their families. They had to discover a new kind of dream beyond the American Dream of achieving individual success. They are now both committed to the dream of seeing their own communities succeed, and they both attest that this dream is much more satisfying than their old dreams were. Moving in other directions, both Chuck and Nico found themselves in a position to touch the lives of children, and they have both set out to give children the tools they will need for a successful life.

While Vernon and Portia continued to foster children, they learned a universal truth about children: "We've had a lot of children come into our home. We've had teenagers. We've had young children. We've had white children. We've had black children. We've had Mexican children. When they need a hug, when they need an embrace, when they need an assurance that their world is going to be okay, that hug doesn't have a color. Those arms that reach around them and the arms that reach back are not black hands, it's not Mexican hands, it's not white hands. It's hands that hold them," Vernon said.

The Padgetts and Venturas both realized that, even though they did not have the kind of success they had always wanted, sometimes we can invest in our futures with something other than money. We all have time to give, and where better to give our time than to our children, who will live in the future we shape today?

Struggle

The Padgetts

When the economy began to collapse, construction companies were among those hardest hit. Finding any way to cut costs became essential. While Chuck had invested years in building a multitude of relationships with many construction companies, those companies stopped calling him. Chuck spoke with a few of his most trusted business associates and asked why he was not getting jobs anymore. His friend replied that it was just business. The friend then revealed that Chuck's bids were being undercut and explained that unless he started offering more competitive prices he would not get the work he needed This did not make sense to Chuck. He had spent years building a successful business, and he was now not only running a stucco company but had also become his own supplier so that he bought his materials direct from the wholesaler. How could anyone afford to underbid him? He was giving his best prices, and he needed the jobs.

Even though the housing market was faltering, Chuck noticed there were still enough jobs in the area to sustain his company. He simply was not getting them. Chuck also started to notice that all employed crews were composed entirely of Hispanics. In fact, some of these laborers had worked for him in the past and had even learned the trade from him. After Chuck inquired a bit more, it became apparent that the crews being hired over his were made up entirely of undocumented workers. Chuck knew now how he was being undercut. These crews did not have to pay insurance, workers compensation, etc. They did not have to file with the government, nor did they have to meet the standards and safety requirements with which his business had to comply or face fines. All of his extra expenses were figured into Chuck's basic costs. The competition could offer lower prices because they did not have to have the overhead that was legally required of Chuck's company.

If his business was under constant scrutiny by the government, it would make sense, Chuck thought, for the same government agencies to perform due diligence in shutting down illegal operations that failed to comply with business regulations and remit the necessary fees. When government inspectors came to his job sites, however, they often drove right past the crew of undocumented workers down the street and came directly for Chuck, writing him fines for any minor infraction they could find. How could this be?

Chuck had had enough. He went to the inspector's headquarters and demanded a meeting. Sitting in the inspector's office, Chuck asked the man why he overlooked the undocumented workers and came after him alone. According to Chuck, the inspector pointed to a filing cabinet behind him and told Chuck it was full of citations against undocumented crews, but all these were unsettled claims. The inspector told Chuck that he could not go after them because there was no way to enforce the fine.

The inspector's job was to collect money for his department, but pursuing undocumented workers proved time and again to be a dead end. The addresses he got for their businesses turned out to be false, and as soon as they finished one job, they moved, especially if they knew the government was watching them. According to Chuck, the inspector looked him in the eye and said, "But, I know where I can find you. I can get your money."

Chuck and Kathy could see the writing on the wall. Their business was about to go under, and there was nothing they could do to prevent its descent. "It was hard to watch, because there was nothing you could do about it, and the government was not helping," Kathy said. Chuck added that all that had been done was done for their dream, the American dream, but soon the undocumented competition "took that away from us as they came in and was able to work as undocumented workers. That started taking our American Dream away from us." Chuck knew the economy was rocky anyway, but he is convinced to this day that he could have held on if he had not been undercut so often.

The first thing Chuck had to do was begin letting employees go. Some of the men who had worked for Chuck as many as twenty years were the first to go because they were the crew leaders making the most money. If Chuck was going to keep the business, he would have to keep the hourly wage workers who were actually doing the physical labor. He could not afford so many managers. "They were like family to us," Chuck said. "They were so angry. There were some that broke into our shop, cut into my safe, and just tore the shop apart and busted windows out of my truck and stuff like that." It angered Chuck, because he knew he had had no choice. On the other hand, he understood why they were so angry. Just like Chuck and Kathy, "they had put their life into this situation as well. Not just us. They had put their time and their life into this business as well. And to this day, there are some of them that won't even speak to me," Chuck lamented.

Chuck became emotional at this point. He recalled times when these friends went through other tough situations, the loss of a family member, for example, and Chuck wanted to be there for them, but he couldn't. He and Kathy were no longer welcome in their lives. Chuck and Kathy were not just losing a business. They were losing friends who had become as dear as family.

Kathy shared with us what she considers perhaps the biggest blow of all, losing the house. "People make fun of us. They mock us." Perhaps no one means to be cruel, but people tend to make remarks when one has to move from a seven thousand square foot home to a doublewide trailer. Even though Kathy still feels a little shame in going back to life in a trailer, they do still have a home. The dream of having a comfortable home where their family can feel safe is not lost because that home is now a trailer. The lawn is well groomed, the interior of the home itself is inviting and extremely tidy. Though not the fulfillment of a childhood dream that was theirs for a while, their home is still a place of peace, a haven beyond alcoholism and abuse, a place the grandchildren still love to visit.

****

At the same time Chuck was losing his business, the private school upon whose board he served was having a rough time as well. The school needed to replace its principal, and, for a time, the board could not find a suitable candidate. With all that was going on in his life, Chuck still volunteered to sit in the principal's office, field calls, and essentially run the school until they could find a suitable replacement. Chuck was simultaneously doing all he could to keep his business afloat. He was offering the lowest prices he could, but the work was simply not there. Instead of sitting around and waiting fruitlessly, he decided to utilize the administrative skills he had developed over two decades of running a business.

Chuck admitted that at times he asked himself what the point of continuing was, but the work ethic his mother had instilled in him would not allow him to be idle, even during a time when work was unavailable. Unlike many private schools, this school's student body was diverse, and the children it served were thriving because of the extra care they received. Many did not come from affluent homes but from homes that valued small class settings and the attention given at such a school. Now, however, their hopes and dreams were in jeopardy. Many families at this school had been receiving financial assistance, but such help was becoming impossible. The economy was taking its toll here as well. Chuck knew the school was in trouble, and he did not want to see any more dreams crash during the economic crisis.

Chuck was not the biggest fan of school when he was growing up, and he had never dreamed of running a center for education. Chuck was a working class man, but after years of learning to run a business from scratch, Chuck had a knack for administration. He would leave the educating to the educators, and he would focus on making sure the school functioned like a well-oiled machine. He was not really looking for a new career but he was prepared to offer his help, even when he was most in need. If this meant that he would also cut the grass, scrub toilets, and repair the roof, he was willing.

After several months of service, the Board of Directors called Chuck in to announce they had found their permanent principal. Chuck was happy to pass the torch to whomever the board had found worthy. When they offered him the position permanently, Chuck was reluctant at first, but the board convinced him he was the man for the job. He was not there for any other reason than to see the school succeed, and even though he was not an educator himself, he did know how to lead, even if his crew was now a group of capable teachers. Soon after Chuck took a permanent position, the board also hired Kathy to run the front office. Once again, Chuck and Kathy were working side by side. They have been married for thirty-two years, and they have worked together thirty of those years. The school now thrives under the leadership of the Padgetts.

The Venturas

It was obvious for our team that what occupied Nico and Dalila's hearts the most, what they were constantly thinking about even more than the possibility of deportation or the dangers they face here, were their families back home. Dalila told us a day doesn't go by that she does not think of her "happy family." Even though her family of five lived in a one-room building and her father was a peasant farmer, she says they were always filled with joy. Her father worked in the fields planting and picking beans, but when they were all together, they would sing. Music brought them together and kept their spirits high. Dalila's job was to help her father in the fields, and to pass the time, they would sing together. Even in their poverty, music always made her happy. Still, it was not enough. Her love for her family compelled her to make the sacrifice to leave to see if she could find a way to help.

Nico speaks a lot of his mother and tells of how much she means to him. After talking of his father's death, Nico took a moment to reflect upon the impact that event had upon his thoughts of the future, "The thought of not seeing my mother ever again is hard. I can't even think about it. I mean, I would—I don't know what I would do. She has always been my strength. She's a very wise woman. She has an answer for everything I ask, for everything in life. She's a godly woman. She's wakes up early in the morning to pray for all her kids. I just don't think—I don't think I can—I don't think I can let her go."

Even though it seems impossible, somewhere deep inside Nico knows that he is going to have the opportunity to go home one day. Something is going to change in the laws to make it easier to visit her while she continues to age: "The memories I have of my mother are so many. She was always working. She was working all the time, her and my dad, but mostly her. She was a hard worker. She did everything she could. She would go without eating so we could eat. She did everything to provide for us, you know, but at the same time, where we're from, it's really hard to find jobs close by. So, she would travel, just looking for places to work. A lot of times we were left home alone for long periods of time, you know, just so she could work. We all see her as a hero."

In addition to his mother, Nico has several sisters who still live with his mother, and when he was growing up, it was their job to raise him: "They are basically the ones that raised me. I'm one of the youngest, so me and my brother were always the babies of the house. We had five mothers, four sisters and a mother. Not having my mom there because she was working, my sisters took the role of mother to us. They are all wonderful. I miss them very much. I have more memories with them than my parents, sadly, because they were working. My sisters are the one's that taught us everything. They are wonderful."

We realized that for our team to really understand Nico's background, we would have to see the things he described for us. We would have to see the conditions he left behind, as well as the family. Why did he leave this family that he cannot refrain from mentioning constantly, no matter what the topic of discussion might be? So we packed our gear and flew out. We landed in a remote area of Mexico and then rented cars to go even deeper into the country.

When we arrived in Nico's hometown, we began to understand what he meant. It was a cinderblock and plywood town. Each business was thrown together with the cheapest grade of plywood available and painted a variety of colors. Around the town were various villages, where many of the homes were made of cinder block. There were probably more unfinished block buildings than finished ones. Sometimes what seemed to be whole neighborhoods of buildings consisted of small buildings with concrete walls that went up four feet or so with no roof and no construction crew in sight to finish the project. Whole sections of never completed domiciles were completely abandoned.

We tried to remain as unobtrusive as possible for a while because we did not want to cause a stir. This area of Mexico does not have a lot of white visitors, especially white visitors with video cameras. Eventually Nico's brother-in-law tracked us down and took us to the home where we would conduct our interview.

"This is all I have," Nico's mother said without despair or sadness. She was simply stating a fact, but it is a fact that many of us will never understand. Most of us will never know what it is like to stand on a packed dirt floor inside a cinderblock room and say, "This is my home. This is everything I own."

The home is, by modern standards, unfinished. Rebar juts out of the walls, bare wire and bulbs crisscross as they dangle from the ceiling. A single sheet of pressed ply board separates the kitchen from the bedroom.

The concrete house has its advantages and

disadvantages. In the middle of a blistering hot day, the dark rooms remain cool, supported by a constant breeze blowing through the windows. The windows were not simply open but paneless. Of course the lack of window panes allows the dust from the dirt road, which is only a few feet from the house, to waft in as cars and semi-trucks speed by, but having the breeze is too important to worry about blocking the dust.

The same concrete that insulates the family from the heat, amplifies the constant cacophony of barking dogs, crowing roosters, and engines. Noise from loud speakers blaring political ads reverberate off the walls of the small room. Even so, a baby being passed about from one family member to the next sleeps soundly while each moves about preparing lunch.

The food is pungent. The dried fish is swarming with flies, and the beef is grey and tough. The most surprising item on the table, however, is not the low quality meat, but the array of fresh vegetables purchased from the local market that morning. How does such fresh produce make it to the middle of this Mexican desert? It makes a beautifully vibrant salsa.

Nico's mother shares her home, which is attached to an old minimart no longer in business, with her daughters. The family has recently acquired the building, not without much help from the money Nico sends back, and has converted it into a home for one of the sisters and her several children. The outside of the home still advertises various food items and drinks that were once sold within, but no one would mistake it as a still thriving business. The inside is fairly spacious but quite bare. All that belongs to the mother and her daughters fits on an old shelving unit that belonged to the minimart before it closed. At the back of the old store is one more concrete room, which appears to have once been the minimart's storage room. It is now the home of the second daughter and her five children. They share one bed, and dirty laundry is stacked in various piles against the wall.

Once lunch is over, it is time for work. The elderly matriarch moves about her yard preparing for a day of laundering clothes. She moves slowly. Her darkened skin and lined face attest that she has walked beneath this desert sun countless times before.

Life moves on for Nico's family. They are able to cope with life in their village more comfortably now because of Nico's contributions, yet Nico cannot see just how much he has contributed and continues to contribute to their welfare because at least for now, he must stay away so that he does not forfeit his ability to provide.

After seeing Nico's village firsthand, we saw just how inadequate his words were to explain his past desperation when he decided to leave for the U.S. and his present desperation to make sure his children don't have to grow up in a place where he has no chance of providing for them what they have in America, much less what they dream of having in the future. As much as they miss their families, Nico and Dalila have no options unless they are willing to give up the stability they have here, even if that stability is relative only to just how easily they could be deported.

Building up others

The Padgetts

While they miss the big house and the large income, the Padgetts seem very fulfilled. It does not take long to notice that they are right where they are supposed to be. In fact, Chuck looks back on his life and believes everything that happened before was grooming him to be the leader he is today. Both he and Kathy have a soft spot for any child in need. They know what it is like to be hungry, and even though their school is a private school, they serve children who are not wealthy at all. Many families scrape to send their children to this school, and they do so because it provides a wonderful environment. Sometimes Kathy works behind the scenes for those struggling to pay tuition. She even has a drawer of food for the kids she notices have nothing at break time. She pulls them aside to avoid embarrassing them and lets them choose a treat. Sometimes Kathy gives families extensions when they cannot pay, and Chuck occasionally takes fire for Kathy's compassion, but he knows from his own experience that frequently, all people need is a chance, an opportunity to make something happen. More often than not, when Kathy offers an extension, the parents are able to repay. It just takes mercy.

The Padgetts now spend most of their time with these families, many of whom are still struggling to regain what they lost in the economic crash themselves. The Padgetts use their experience to help people find meaning beyond the money. They give whenever possible to keep tuition low, not because they are again trying to save a business. "It's not about the money," Kathy says. Instead, it is about building people up and setting children up with an education that will propel them into a greater future.

The Padgetts live for this community, and they develop a deep love for every child who passes through their doors. They do not dwell on the past. They still hope that our government will find a way to make the American Dream more stable so that others won't fall victim to the same heartbreak, but they hold no grudges. They know that each person who took a job away from them was a person also trying to provide for his own as well. Chuck and Kathy now live to help those looking for a better future find it through education and community.

The Venturas

After one of our visits to the Ventura home, we sat outside the modest, creaky singlewide trailer to watch the children play. Dalila made us a delicious meal, and we all relaxed, except for Nico. He was setting up for his class. One after another, Hispanic families pulled into the front yard and dropped off their little ones, who hopped out with an instrument in hand. Nico is a musician, and he has always dreamed of using his talent to bless others.

Nico knows how people perceive undocumented workers. He has been treated like a criminal more times than he cares to recall. He remembers one occasion when his family went out to eat at a local restaurant and spoke Spanish to one another at the table. The people at the table next to theirs must have assumed Spanish was their only language, because they started speaking about Nico's family, and not in hushed tones. Nico did not want to tell us what they said. Dalila stepped in to say only that their words were horrible. Nico said it was heartbreaking because his children could hear as well, but he told them in Spanish not to react. He never let the people speaking about his family know he understood because he did not want to create a scene. He instructed the children to try to ignore the unkindness and enjoy their meals.

Even so, he wished people could know the real Nico, whose deepest dream is to be a part of his community. He and Dalila have already sacrificed so much community by leaving their families so that they know the value of belonging to something greater than oneself. Nico wants to make meaningful relationships with his new community. Contrary to what some may assume, he did not remain in the U.S. only because he wants to take from this country. He genuinely wants to give back, and, in what he assumes to be a small way, he has.

Nico began to watch a pattern emerge among the Hispanic children with whom he came into contact every week at church. He noticed that once children reached legal age and were no longer under the custody of their parents, they disappeared from the community. He wondered what sort of life these youth were moving into. What was it that they were learning about from their peers that would draw them away from home?

About six months ago, Nico was speaking to the middle school children at his church and overheard them talking about things of which he did not expect children their age to be aware. He asked them if they knew what drugs were, and they did. They knew very well. This frightened Nico. They had learned about drugs at school, the same school Nico and Dalila's two girls now attend. Nico wanted to do something to help these children find the right path, something they could set their minds on so they would know they had other options in life.

Nico began to wonder what he could offer them: "I learned to play guitar when I was 14 years old and, ever since then, I love music. It's what kept me from many things. It occupies your mind. It keeps your mind healthy. So, I talk to my wife and told her about what I was thinking. I talk to the kids and asked them if they wanted to learn how to play music. They were all excited. So, six months ago, we started."

Nico and Dalila meet several of the local children at the church, and each gets an instrument. They learn to play praise songs together. Nico has seen children, even with the worst behavioral problems, blossom in his program. Nico knows there are so many other kids outside his local Hispanic church community who face the same issues every day. He also knows this is not an issue exclusive to one race or ethnicity, and he dreams of a community wide program that welcomes all children to discover their talents.

Nico, however, cannot offer his services to the surrounding community as he does for other Hispanics in his own circle because he is undocumented and must remain in the shadows. He wants to make a difference in the lives of more children, to lead them to a better life. Ironically, he is limited in leading children away from a life of crime because he is considered a criminal himself. For now, Nico will continue to dream of giving back. He and Dalila long for the day when, as Dalila put it, people will see them as equal persons: "We have love, we have family. We are the same."

"We do not want to take from this country. We love this country," Nico said. Nico and Dalila now dream of what they can do for others. They continue to build family here with other Hispanics, but that is not where they wish to stop. They gather with other Hispanics with the same dream of giving back to America, and they all hope that one day they can leave the shadows to have such an opportunity.

Chapter Eight:

"Pressing Forward to What Lies Ahead"

For Drew and Meagan, guiding their families forward as Christian leaders means focusing on what lies ahead. This does not, however, mean leaving the past behind, but using the past, with all its struggles and pain, to help others in their time of need.

Vernon knows a thing or two about loving others after pain. He even knows what it means to love people who have caused him pain: "The scars have really never gone. I am healed in that when you've been hurt that hard, that deep, and you recover, your love is bullet proof. That power I have is to love my neighbor."

Portia added, "My love for you will outshine your hate for me." Love is powerful, and it is the only thing that can outmatch pain, and even hate. Both the Thompsons and the Hodges use their past hurt to feed their love and not their hate. This is a choice, and it is a beautiful one from which we can learn.

The Thompsons

The Thompsons were not in a big rush to start a family. They had each other, and that was enough, especially since their plans were going to take them a long way from their hometowns and families. Drew wanted to go to seminary, and Mandy, as always, was behind him the whole way. Moving to Boston, Drew and Mandy knew that seminary was supposed to be an intense experience. Drew was focused on school, and Mandy was making just enough money to support their dreams. Having a child was not at the top of their list.

They did talk from time to time about expanding their family, but Mandy has never been one to take the conventional path: "That didn't matter to me. I think it's important and beautiful for people, but I also think that having unconventional avenues of creating a family is also beautiful and wonderful. So, we did consider an adoption from early on." It was always something they wanted to do.

Still, the adoption process is a long road. It requires a lot of money and time, neither of which were resources readily available during their time in seminary. Adoption would have to wait until they moved back home and obtained full time jobs, so they decided to begin their family through conception. This process proved to be an even longer road for the couple, one full of heartbreak and confusion. They realized after a few months that things were not working out as they had hoped. Their doctor told them that these things sometimes take a while, and though there might be some complications, they needed to give it a year before having the battery of tests that await people struggling with infertility. A year did pass, and they found out that there were issues, but the doctors held out hope and put Mandy on fertility medication that worked.

Though Mandy had wondered if she would have that motherly instinct, as soon as she found out there was a life inside of her, "that Mama Bear in me was automatic." Mandy was determined to protect her child at all costs. She would now live and die for her baby.

Eventually, Mandy began to feel that something was wrong. Though she had never been pregnant before, she knew instinctively what was happening. She was having a miscarriage. The physical and emotional toll of this experience was devastating. Mandy explained that society does not give much thought to miscarriage. Drew admitted that they had had friends go through miscarriages from time to time, and it was never really something they thought much about, but when it happened to them, they realized all the things that people miss about the truth of miscarriage, especially the silent suffering.

Many couples who experience such loss often go on to have successful pregnancies, but some, like Drew and Mandy, eventually have to accept that they will not. Compounding their sorrow is their lack of a way to commemorate this life. Usually, loved ones have a time to gather to grieve and remember, a time to experience support and understanding from others. For Mandy, there was no such commemoration for her loss. There was no ceremony, no grave marker. Nothing. Many people never even knew so that while well-intentioned people continued to ask when they were ever going to get started on having a family, Mandy and Drew had to put on a brave face and carry on as if nothing had happened. They simply smiled and said, "Soon."

Their pain was so great that it challenged this couple at a spiritual level, especially Mandy, but in many ways, while it has totally reoriented the way she looks at faith, she finds her faith to be stronger. Ironically, this does not mean that she has now more answers than she did before. In fact, she has less. All the nice, cozy sentiments we express to one another in times of grief really do not deal with the root of our pain. Through confronting the pain and acknowledging that answers are not easy nor always complete, Mandy has learned to lean more on trust than on self:

"Going through infertility and a miscarriage was an identity crisis. It was more than that; it was a spiritual crisis for me. There are certain things that happen in life that you just can't understand. You can be mad as hell about it. You can shake your fists at heaven. That doesn't make these things go away. It is just life, and I don't fully understand it. I think that pretty answers negate the pain and negate the struggle. I think slapping a coat of white paint on pain does not really make it go away. It just makes it harder to see. But you can't come out the other side unless you truly look at it and you truly see it. So we have to face those things in life that make us ache, that make us question. I don't have many answers. The further I live my life, the further I look deeply at my faith, the less answers I have and the more questions I have, but I'm growing very comfortable with those questions. I'm realizing that is an ironic part of the beauty of peace and grace and faith that we have to reach beyond the lack of answers, we have to cross that divide with our souls and just say a quiet 'yes.' We can't avoid pain if you're truly living. If you're truly showing up for life, you can't avoid pain. So, the best thing that you can do is work with what you've been given."

Drew processed his grief in a much different manner than Mandy, but he did so, just like Mandy, through the lens of faith. The God whom he had avoided as a younger man, the God others portrayed as real and really there, was now being made manifest in the way he had only dreamed. He thought his relationship with God was going to be more of a natural process than this. He had already dedicated his life to ministry and study, but it was in grief that he felt God was truly with him.

He thought frequently about Jesus' many statements about the pains of life. He knew that while many wanted Jesus when all was just right, Jesus was not there for the good times alone, nor was he there to make life good all the time. He was to be there for Drew in the darkest times. For Drew, this was it. It was time to test this faith. Was Jesus going to be there for him? "Before this time, there were a lot of things that did not make sense. I had a good life," Drew said. Sure, he had believed all the statements about Jesus' being for the hurting and the needy, but he had not understood them experientially until now. His faith became ever more real in his pain. During a time of senseless loss, Drew found something that made sense: "He was there all along, and I said, 'Yep, this is it.'"

The miscarriage broke Drew's heart too, but not in the same way it impacted Mandy's. She, after all, had carried the child and experienced the physical bond of pregnancy. Drew dealt with his grief by focusing on his studies, but Mandy slipped into a deep depression, "...the don't get out of bed depression," Mandy said. In fact, she was so paralyzed by her pain that she almost lost her job. She had to pull herself together and bury her grief deep down just so that they could get through seminary. She did not realize how much pain she was suppressing until they finally moved back home, where she was finally able to grieve and find support when she found it was okay to share. Of course, other people had miscarriages and remained silent, but that did not mean she couldn't talk about hers. That healing process, Mandy told us, was not without much pain. There is still pain today. I could hear it in every word as she shared her story; however, she was eventually able to discuss the possibility of adoption with Drew again.

****

Considering the extent of their pain, it is hard to believe that the Thompsons would invite the emotional risks involved in foster care, but that is the pathway to parenthood they chose. Through their struggles to enlarge their family, the Thompsons had begun to realize the beauty that can come from pain. After they had examined all their options, domestic and international, they told a close friend they did not care what child they received. Race did not matter. Age did not matter. All that mattered was the love they had to give, and all they wanted was a child who really needed that love.

Their friend suggested they consider using The Department of Family and Children Services as their avenue. Because the department was in great need of assistance, not only would they be helping a child, but they would also be helping a network of people who dedicate their lives to displaced children every day.

The issue, of course, was that the state's first priority is to restore families, not create new ones. If there was any chance a child or children could return to their parents, the foster parents would have to release the children who had become a part of their home, no questions asked. Drew and Mandy had asked DFCS to help them find a child in most need and parents who were leaning toward giving their child up for adoption. Even so, there was always the chance of having to give the child back. They chose this road, not because it was easy, but because it was where they saw the greatest need. This can only be a testimony of the faith journey they were traveling and the strength it imbued.

The process was long and invasive. The state wanted to be sure that any foster home it approved was capable of providing a stable environment for children who had been removed from all that they knew. The months continued to pass with many interviews and home visits, but no word on a child. Finally, the Thompsons received the phone call for which they had waited so long. By the time the twin girls arrived at the Thompsons' home, they had been in foster care for over half of their lives. It was love at first sight. From the moment they first saw the girls, Drew and Mandy knew they would be willing, if the opportunity came, to be the children's "forever family." Still, they had balance their hopes with the possibility that they would someday have to give the children back to the state to be rejoined with their original family no matter what.

Eventually, Drew and Mandy learned that the courts had terminated the parental rights of the biological family so that the girls were available for adoption. The Thompsons immediately filed all the paper work and attended all the court hearings. Sixteen months ago, Drew and Mandy became the twins' forever parents and gave them a forever home.

Speaking about her two life changing events at once, Mandy recalls, "I can't imagine it being any other way and the girls that we have are about the same age as that child would've been, by about a month. So, I have two now instead of one, and it's beautiful. But beauty doesn't come without pain, and life, life and love don't come without pain."

When we asked Drew and Mandy to describe these two six-year-old girls they now call their own, they did not say very much, nor did they need to in order to prove how much they adore their girls. The Thompsons' feelings were more evident in how they interacted with their daughters than in what the couple said. Watching the family together gave us a picture of who the Thompsons are as a family. Dad is a thinker, Mom is an artist, and the girls are explorers, and life is an adventure. Because the foster program holds foster parents to high standards of confidentiality, Drew and Mandy were not allowed to share pictures or much information at all about the girls. Drew and Mandy saw how vulnerable their girls were when they first came to them, and they continue to protect them in this regard.

As was also the case at the Jackson's home, the Thompsons did not allow us to capture the girls' faces. They did, however, allow us simply to watch their family. Drew and Mandy are parents to the core. They are not distracted by work, by phones, or by little mishaps. They hang on to every word the girls say. They let them know they are heard, and they also direct the girls' paths by giving them a new foundation upon which to thrive.

It was faith that brought them to this point as a family, and Drew and Mandy feel honored and obligated to continue in that faith and to raise their girls in the faith they so desperately needed to grow their forever beautifully mismatched family tree.

The Hodges

Megan and Desiree met at Fort Stewart and began hanging out as friends in 2009. Megan was drawn to Desiree because of Desiree's personality. While most people on base were naturally drawn to the chaplain, especially since she always carried snacks and other goodies to build soldiers' morale, Desiree, shy and stoic, was not as quick to come running to Megan. Megan noticed, however, that Desiree treated other soldiers with compassion and wondered what made her this way. After she found out Desiree was gay, Megan wanted to know about Desiree's faith. Desiree had struggled with the faith of her upbringing, as had Megan and they found a confidante to whom each could talk about her faith and her personal struggles in an authentic way in each other.

Desiree told us her deep feelings for Megan began to develop when Megan cared for her after she had hurt her feet while practicing for a long running competition at the base. Megan purchased materials to bandage Desiree's feet, and Desiree knew it was not simply because Megan was the chaplain. Rather, Megan's motivation was genuine care for a friend.

Megan had dated other women before, but none of them proved to be the person with whom she wanted to have a permanent relationship. Desiree was different, and Megan knew this meant that someday, she would have to share her relationship with her parents. She feared the revelation would do irrevocable damage to the family bond she had so treasured for years. At first, she had decided to hide her orientation from her parents forever. She thought that if someone had to suffer, she would rather it be her, but now, to be fair to both her family and Desiree, she knew she would have to tell her parents the truth eventually.

****

Megan believes that for most people in the LGBT community, being gay is not as much about making a decision as it is about making a discovery. "Love is a very hard thing to control," Megan told us. For Megan, being gay is not really about sex but about where her love directs itself. "I think a lot of people have a very hard time understanding that being gay has nothing to do with the sex. It really is about your affection." To help us understand what she meant by this, Megan asked us to think about all the straight couples we know. She asked us what the first thing that came into our minds was when we thought of all those couples. "When somebody says they're straight, you think about it very much in terms of a noun. 'Yeah, you're straight.'" For men, Megan illustrated, "You think about their wife and kids. You don't think—at least I don't, maybe people do— I don't think, 'Oh, what do they do sexually together?' That's not even a thought that enters my mind." However, Megan believes that when many people find out someone they know is gay, they immediately think about sex. If someone were to ask Megan and Desiree about their lives, Megan said, he or she would probably find it kind of boring. Most of the time, according to Megan, they are just like everyone else; they just sit around and watch Netflix.

For Megan, coming to the realization that she was gay was so much more complicated than discovering her sexual preferences. She had to comprehend a network of feelings for the same sex. Megan recalled the first time she discovered there might be something a bit different with the way she thought compared to what is considered the norm. She was riding in the car with her older brothers, who were having a conversation, and Megan, hanging onto every word as usual, overheard one say to the other while he pointed out a girl, "Oh, man! She's a fox!" Megan, wanting to participate in the conversation, remarked without a second thought, "Oh, yeah! She is a fox!" As Megan recalls, her brothers had the reaction most boys would. They both snapped their heads around toward the back seat and told her that she could not say things like that because it was gross.

After being scolded for her transgression, Megan was flooded with emotion. Only a child, she had meant nothing sexual. How could she? She was in no way interested in sex. She thought she was simply admiring beauty; however, this was the first time she realized there was a social expectation that she not admire the same sex in such a way, even though she really did inside.

When Megan reached her early teens, she began to discover that her appreciation for women was perhaps more intense than she had assumed. "I would find myself thinking a lot about particular girls and trying to figure out, 'Is this how you feel about normal friends?'" Megan, like many adolescents, spent her early teen years in inner dialogue. She would lie awake at night and wonder why her mind drifted to the girls in her life and not the boys. "I can remember a few older ladies in my life that were mentor figures, and when I look back now, it's like, 'Duh!' I had a crush on them.'" Megan recalls that at first she could not identify what was going on, but when she reached 16, she finally realized what was happening, and she panicked: "Oh, no. What now?"

Growing up while knowing she was different was very hard on Megan. "I think there's probably a good majority of the LGBT community who has, at some point, thought about suicide. I know the thought crossed my mind, but my faith was really the anchor that prevented me from going any further than that." Megan told us that the real struggle was the loneliness. Trying to make it real to us when we interviewed her, Megan gave us another illustration: "You probably remember what it's like to have that first boyfriend or girlfriend. You end up breaking up, and you're so heartbroken over your first love. You could talk to your friends and tell them, 'Aw, man, she hurt me so bad,' or 'he hurt me so bad,' but when you are gay and no one can know, and you are heartbroken, because you're an adolescent teenager, and you're emotionally unprepared, you deal with all your grief yourself." Megan told us this isolation is simply devastating.

She also explained that if people who bring guilt and shame into the conversation knew the affect it had on children, they would probably stop or at least approach the topic another way because this is not only a matter of right and wrong, but also a matter concerning the emotional welfare of real people, specifically children. No one should want children struggling with their sexual identity to feel so ostracized that they have to keep their feelings a secret. To tell children who feel a certain way they had better get over whatever is haunting them on their own or be the scorn of society cannot be the right way to approach this, but because many are not willing to have a conversation about sexuality, this is exactly what happens.

The results of such silence are devastating. Members of the LGBT community have ended up on the streets because they were not welcome in their own homes: "It is absolutely devastating what we allow to happen to human beings, to *human beings*. We're not talking about stray animals. We are talking about human beings," Megan said.

Megan was successful at covering up what was going on inside for years at great personal expense. On the outside she appeared to be the perfect model of what those around her expected, but on the inside she suffered torment. When it came to boys, Megan would go on dates with friends, but she would use her Christian faith as the excuse she needed to avoid unwanted contact with the opposite sex: "*I'm a Christian*. It was such a perfect cover. I do feel bad for the guys I dated, but it was such a good cover to be the good Christian girl." On one level, Megan liked the admiration others had for her purity, and she knew it was right from her perspective regardless of whether or not she also used it as an excuse, but she knew that on some level, she was not being good simply to be good. She was also trying to bury this inner conflict with a crutch. According to Megan, her faith community should have been all the crutch she needed, but she did not have the outside support she desired, so she turned to an inauthentic way of dealing with her angst: hiding

On the inside, Megan was in pain. She had no one but God to talk to: "It was this forbidden thing. I can remember going to Christian youth camps and being at the altar and weeping, 'God, take this away. God, why is this such an issue?' There would be these moments where I would think, 'Okay, I'm not gay any more. God didn't make me gay.'" At this age, Megan thought it was as simple as behavior modification. She was not going to do anything that was considered gay. She was not going to hold another girl's hand. She would not kiss a girl, and so on, and this would solve the issue. But, there was one problem: "My affections and heart did not change at all." The "fake it till you make it" model was just not going to work in this case, but Megan was not going to quit pursuing this solution without a fight. Her determination to deny her feelings began at youth camp, and she continued a pattern of refusing herself any physical acts with the same sex while trying to date members of the opposite sex to whom she was in no way attracted throughout college and seminary.

According to Megan, she had to call it quits, at least in part, by the time she had completed her first year in the military. She felt that she was lying to all the people she was trying to help by not admitting to her own struggles. Megan chose for a time to remain single. She was constantly asked why she wasn't dating, when she was going to get married, how many kids she planned to have, and the like, but she thought it better to have people wonder why she was single than to continue dating people for whom she had no affection. It was not fair to her or the men she tried to date.

****

Megan knew telling her parents would be devastating for them, "I can remember when I was young, that song "Butterfly Kisses" came out. I can remember mom saying, 'Oh, I can't wait for this to play while Dad is walking you down the aisle.' I know there had to be a part of my parents that hoped for the traditional son-in-law." Megan knew telling her parents she was gay might not only anger them because of their beliefs, but also crush their dreams.

Megan was beginning to cope with her sexuality, but she was slow to tell others. She had lived a life in which she allowed others to think she was something she was not, and her selfless nature led her to feel grief over having to let them down. When she finally told her parents, though she had known the day was coming, the conversation was not planned. It just happened. Her parents knew Desiree, but Megan had introduced her under the pretense of mere friendship. From 2010 to the end of 2012, Megan kept her relationship with Desiree from them, but the emotions kept building and in what began as an ordinary conversation with her mother, Megan finally told the truth.

It was a busy day. Megan and her parents were working hard to get Megan's cabin on the market. While Megan and her mother, Vicky, were inside packing boxes, Megan's father, Eric, was outside doing yard work. Megan and her mother were having a normal conversation to pass the time while they did their busy work. As is often typical for daughters who are close to their mothers, Megan was telling her mom stories involving her friends, but for her mom, the conversation was anything but typical. Something about it seemed a bit strange. Vicky recalled the moment she confronted Megan, "It seemed to me most all of her friends were lesbians, and I said, 'Megan, are you gay?' She just broke down. We just held each other. I guess I had suspected it for a while. Afterwards she just kept saying she was sorry that she didn't tell me, but she said she was so afraid that her dad and I would not love her anymore."

Vicky came outside and motioned for Eric, who was enjoying his work outdoors, to come in. Seeing the worried look on his wife's face, Eric couldn't imagine what she was about to say: "My first thought was that my sweatshirt and jeans did not match." Apparently, Eric was always getting in trouble for not dressing properly, even when doing yard work. But as he got closer to the door, Eric realized something was really wrong. Vicky was in tears.

Eric walked into the cabin to find his daughter broken as he had never seen her before. "When your children hurt, you learn their different cries. You learn the bratty, whiny cry and the bone chilling cry that just gets right to your core." When Eric recalled the story, his voice never broke and he never grimaced, but tears streamed from his eyes.

Eric was having an internal war. On the one hand, his daughter's newly revealed sexuality conflicted with his deepest beliefs about what was best for his child. On the other hand, her cry was speaking to a deepest level of his fatherhood and his need to protect his own. He knew this was not an act of defiance. His daughter was hurting. This was a moment of despair.

Megan's father reacted with shock: "If you would have hit me with a hammer that day, you would've had to tell me you did. I think my first words were 'I don't accept that.' It did not even enter in that it was a possibility," Eric recalled. After the initial shock wore off and Eric rethought his first response, he went back to his devastated daughter and told her, "This is not going to change our relationship." Eric was determined that his family could make it through whatever was ahead. "With God's help, with God's guidance, we're going to tackle this thing, we're going to take it head on." For the remainder of the day, all Eric wanted to do was continue his yard work. He felt numb and needed to process what he had learned before he could continue the conversation.

****

Eric loves his daughter but admitted, "the process I had to go through really, really set me back." Eric prayed and asked God to help him figure out how this wasn't going to tear his family apart. They were and still are a Christian family. Eric and Vicky were not going to change that, and Megan had no plans of leaving the faith either, although some of the friends she came out to told her she should.

Now Eric and Vicky had to learn to support their daughter while balancing that support with their convictions. "God put a mirror up in front of me and said, 'What do you believe?'" For Eric, this was the first time he had ever thought about what it would mean to have a gay child.

Until this time, Eric had never put any real thought into the matter. He knew he believed this lifestyle was not supported by his faith, but now he would have to face the complexity this brings when the issue becomes personal and convictions demanding faithfulness collide. On one hand, he did not believe being gay was best for his daughter. On the other hand, he could tell her emotions were real. The cry he heard the day she told him about her orientation proved that to him. Like any good father, he was dedicated to his daughter, whom he would never hesitate to protect, and now she was in a place where she might find herself scorned by those she loved. He was determined that no scorn would come from her parents despite his convictions.

No longer standing on the outside of this issue, Eric had to consider how to proceed: "I now had to make a decision as the head of the house. As the head of the safe zone, my decisions count. I'm not a spectator in this." Eric began to realize just how thoughtless most people were when dealing with the issue, even himself at times: "It is almost like a sporting event. In sporting events there's winners and losers, and that's the way society deals with it," but now the one feeling like a loser in the game others are playing, others who have no real stake in the outcome, was his daughter.

Eric and Megan agree on one crucial point. They have decided that even if they do not agree, they are going to love each other through this journey. They know this is a difficult issue for others and if they are going to allow people to be authentic, just as Megan was striving to be, they cannot demand they be on the same page: "It's a process," Eric told us. "We all have to get there individually."

For Eric's part, he is still not in full agreement with the way Megan is living her life, but he has reconciled himself to walk this path with her. Vicky has come to see things a bit differently than her husband. She agrees with Megan that her lifestyle is what is best for her. Either way, her parents have continued to welcome Megan into their lives, and because Megan has taken Desiree as her own, they love Desiree as well.

Megan's brothers are on that journey too. Eric and Megan agree that "the boys" love Megan deeply, but her brothers are not ready to take this journey side by side. As men with strong convictions, they are still trying to figure out how they will model their beliefs for their children in this difficult situation. Now that Megan is married to Desiree, coming together means facing the issue head on, and the brothers deserve the time, according to Eric and Megan, to think through their own responsibility to provide a safe place for their children, but acknowledging this does not make the strained family dynamic easier on Megan. "I know they love me," Megan said, "and I love them too, but it's hard to do family holidays. I've pulled back, because it's too hard to not be me, to not be authentic." Megan still stays in touch with the brothers.

When talking of her parents' response, Megan told us, "What I appreciate, and what I appreciate in any disagreement, is the love and grace that they still show. I think that's all any of us are really asking for: Believe and think what you want, but please don't treat me any differently." Megan did not want to be treated like she was now trash, like she had no heart, no conscience. She wanted to be loved, even by people who thought she was wrong, and she did not believe that was too much to ask. Megan's parents, through much wrestling of their own, rose to this occasion and treated Megan as they would have wanted to be treated.

After she came out to the most important people in her life, Megan was finally ready to start the rest of her life with Desiree, and they married in 2013. It was a small ceremony, and their families were not there because they believed it would still be too hard on everyone. Among Megan's family and friends are still many people who are unwilling to be around Megan and Desiree. It is a tough place, but it is made a little more comfortable knowing that Eric and Vicky have made space, despite the disagreements still between them, to allow Megan and Desiree into their lives.

The Thompsons

Drew admitted that on one level, he wants to be a student of what is going on in the nation. He believes that state sanctioned civil unions allowing people to file jointly as a family unit and permitting hospital visits for whomever the hospitalized individual considers a life partner is a topic we need to discuss as a nation.

On the other hand, as a pastor and leader of a local church, there is a different set of rules by which he must abide, the rules set forth in Scripture: "Christianity is not about rights; it's about grace." For Drew, that grace comes when a Christian submits to the ways of Christ outlined by Scripture, the grace that got him through his journey. It is not a grace he wants to force on anyone, but it is a grace that he will share with any who call him their pastor. For his church, as is the case for many evangelical churches, there are standards that go beyond individual state provided rights and freedoms, and these rules he does not feel at liberty to change in any way, including the rules of marriage. "It is a definition I've inherited and I do not feel at liberty to change or alter that in any way…It is my job to safeguard the tradition.

To love Jesus, from Drew's point of view, is to obey Scripture, and, like others, he does not want to be told that he has to love in a different way. Jesus is now as real to him as any other person he loves, if not more so.

Drew firmly believes these rules are not simple impositions given from a deity who wants to see if his subjects will jump through hoops. They are not arbitrary at all. They are given out of love so that if God asks Drew not to do certain things, he will do his best to obey, and as a pastor, lead those under his guidance in the same way. To suggest that he cannot do so would be just as much an infraction on his right to love whom he chooses, even if some think his God is not real, as it would be for him to force civil rules on others about whom they can love based on his convictions. For Drew, obedience to God's loving rules is the best way to love God back, and so he will do so. We must all learn, therefore, to allow others to love whom they choose to love.

Since the formative years of their marriage were largely spent upon the difficult journey of creating family, Drew uses the lens of fatherhood to explain his deepest self. Drew, as a pastor, is charged with the care of his congregation. Much like a father, he has to find the balance between providing his congregation with freedom to be who they are and the constant challenge of respecting the boundaries God has set before them.

For Drew, this means teaching his children, as well as his congregation, that there is a God who loves them, a God who has a plan for them. Just like his girls, many people feel that for most of their lives they have been tossed about as if there is no one out there who really cares. Drew has made it his life's goal to set parameters for his girls that teach them they are loved by their parents and by God and they do have worth. They are not accidents tossed about at the whim of the cosmos.

So, what about those of the LGBT community who come to Drew's church? He is a traditional pastor who believes God's best for us is either heterosexual, monogamous marriage or singleness. How, then, does he relate to those who come in feeling that fate has dealt them a hand they don't know how to handle because society, especially the society of faith, tells them they are an abomination?

Drew explained his approach for us with a hypothetical scenario: " If one of my daughters, and this may happen, came to me in however many years and said, 'Dad, I am gay' or 'Dad, I think I might be gay,' without a doubt, the first thing I would do is hug her. The first thing I would do is remind her of how much I love her and care about her and how what she just told me doesn't change that because you've got to think about what it takes for a daughter to tell her father that. What kind of self-torment, self-confusion, maybe even self-hatred she'd been through, all the messages she's getting from this world, how has she processed this to get to the point? She's been on a journey I haven't even been on." This might seem easy for Drew to say since this hasn't happened, but we must remember that Drew, as a Christian, believes his faith makes him real family with those who call themselves Christian, especially those of his own church.

The Bible has much to say about Christians being

family, and it speaks of family as those adopted by God. As an adoptive father himself, Drew knows adoption means much more than pretending to be family. Adoption is real. For Drew, this is not only an analogy to his faith. Therefore, Drew has had to learn how to have these difficult discussions with his own congregation, which is just like family.

Drew continued, "So the first thing she needs to know is, she's still mine; she's still my daughter and that's never ever going to change, and that I love her and that's never ever going to change. So, that begins a long journey. That begins a journey of finding something new about this person, and how are you going to be a family to them? How are we going to love each other? How are we going to walk together, and how are we going to learn together about this?" I could not help but notice in this moment how much Drew's reflection on what this journey would be like was exactly what Eric had chosen to do. In other words, it is possible. Not without much pain and reflection, but it is possible nonetheless.

"If you don't start there, you don't go anywhere. If she doesn't know in her bones — this is something we tell our girls all the time — when we have to discipline them and they have to go to their room or they have to go to time out or whatever, one of the questions, we always ask them is, 'Do we love you no matter what? Do we love you on good days? Do we love you on bad days?' They're getting to the place — because they used to tell us, 'No, you don't love me when I do this, you don't love me,' which, I get it. But we have to say, 'That's not true. We love you all the time. We love you no matter who you are. We love you just how you are.' That's the only way you're ever going to walk down a road with somebody, because it's going to be a road. It's going to be a journey. You talk about a life changing, life-defining event or characteristic, that's it. So that's the first thing and I think we'd just take it from there."

This is really the crux of the issue for Drew, who, like most parents, knows he has the capability to love unconditionally, even if he doesn't sanction the actions of the one to whom his love is directed. If only the larger Christian community could learn to love in this way, to love in spite of disagreement. If only those on the outside could really understand that disagreement does not mean a lack of compassion and love. It can exist along with the desire for a deep meaningful relationship.

The Hodges

Megan has studied Scripture her whole life, and she knows those passages that speak against sexual immorality. She, however, believes that passages pertaining to homosexuality have been misinterpreted, often because of linguistic and cultural differences that existed when the Bible was written and compiled. While she knew this and had reconciled her decision to be with Desiree to her faith, she also knew that others would not be so open.

One day during a counseling session, Megan realized it was not enough to come out to family and friends. She would have to make her personal life known in her professional life. A female soldier came into her office and sat down. Fidgeting in her chair, she told Megan she had to confess something but already knew what Megan thought of her. When Megan asked how the soldier could possibly know how Megan was going to react to whatever it was the soldier was going to tell her, the soldier lifted her finger and motioned to the cross that hung from Megan's necklace.

She told Megan she really wasn't looking for much advice since she had heard it all before. She just needed a listening ear. "I just got released from the hospital," the soldier informed Megan. She turned over her wrists to show Megan the scars inflicted in a suicide attempt.. "I don't know what to do anymore. I wanted to die." Essentially, she was not telling her chaplain, "I don't know what to do to keep from hurting myself anymore." She was saying, "I had one option, and it failed. "

Reeling at this point, Megan needed more information.

The soldier had come to her office in desperation, though her first choice had been to end her own life. Megan was her second option. Megan, needing more information, asked the girl what it was that made her feel she wanted to end her own life.

The soldier answered, "You can probably already guess, since I told you I know what you think, but I'm gay." Megan knew there was more. A lot of people are gay but do not want to die. She tried to go deeper: "What else?"
The soldier simply added, "And I'm Christian."
Megan could simply reply, "Ah."

After a moment, the soldier continued, "I've tried everything." She told Megan that when she finally told her family, they took her to the church and locked the doors. They were not going to leave until the demon was gone. After hours and hours of prayer she told her family "it" was gone. She was not "cured," she just could not stand being there any longer. They went home, but she did not give up. She continued to pray. She was still praying the day she tried to end her life so that she could be with God instead of with her suffering. She asked God to forgive her for being a sinner, and then she sliced her wrists open while she continued to pray and ask for forgiveness so that she might die in a state of grace because she did not want to go to Hell.

One of the last things she said was, "But I lived and I don't know what to do."

"My worlds collided, because here I am, a closeted chaplain hearing her story," Megan said. "Something had to change," but, at the moment, Megan could not tell her. She could not show her empathy for fear she would be found out herself. Soon, Megan decided to risk the career she loved for the sake of honesty and the ability to be honest with anyone who ever came to her again with such a story.

Megan was heartbroken. The whole reason the chaplaincy exists is to protect a person's first amendment rights, to allow a person to connect with faith in the way that the person sees fit. Here was a soldier who wanted to connect with her faith but felt as if instead, that faith was pushing her off a cliff. Megan knew that perhaps the best thing she could have done in that moment was to tell the soldier her chaplain could relate, but Megan had to leave the soldier in her isolation.

Even though the military no longer limits enlistment based upon sexual orientation, the restrictions for chaplains are a bit more rigorous depending on who endorses that chaplain because a chaplain represents a particular religious institution for soldiers wishing to connect with that religion. Most endorsers, including Megan's, have rules limiting their involvement with the LGBT community. After the Defense of Marriage Act (DOMA) was repealed, according to Megan, the chaplaincy program was inundated with new rules. Many chaplains were not allowed to counsel same sex couples or lead a retreat that allowed same sex couples to participate.

When she looked over the new regulations Megan recalled "feeling completely alone, completely isolated, just hurting so bad because this thing I loved is now leaving a bitter taste in my mouth." Megan knew she had hidden her sexuality from her endorsers, who clearly outlined for Megan the standard of faith to which she was obligated and which disagreed with her being a part of the LGBT community. Overall, she did not blame the institution or its endorsers for upholding those standards, even if their doing so meant she would have to find another endorsement, but she wondered if the strict rules did not limit ministry, even for those who believed in this standard.

Megan wondered if those in charge could ever know what it is like to experience the feelings of the soldier who came to tell her chaplain that her faith was driving her to desperation. She also wondered if the church would be so concerned about making sure that the regulations were clear by drawing firm lines in the sand if it knew that in the meantime people were hurting. Would the faith community really want to limit these people from experiencing what these retreats and other faith building activities have to offer?

After Megan had fallen deeply in love with her job and risen to lead a great ministry with a number of chaplains under her, she finally had to come to terms with who she was. She knew she had to come out. She had made a few very close friends in whom she decided to confide so that she might have some support while she moved forward.

Megan harbors many regrets now for waiting so long to come out. She has realized that hiding her identity from others and being inauthentic hurt her friends when she finally told them the truth. After she told a few people, the news of her sexual orientation rapidly spread to other chaplains, "It was like the spark that started the fire. The fact that I was gay spread in 24 hours. I had people calling me from the East Coast. Two calls came from Hawaii. I had at least fifty people drop me from Facebook. It was pretty shocking. I had some pretty scathing emails, and a lot of the hurtful things were from friends. A handful, literally a handful, I could count on were sticking by me."

The most difficult part of Megan's ordeal was the inability of some who supported her in private to do so in public as well. Professionally, they were in the same place Megan was. They all knew their endorsements as chaplains hung on a standard of faith. Anything deemed dissent could jeopardize that endorsement. That is when Megan hit her lowest point and suffered depression herself. Other soldiers had a chaplain to whom they could turn in their need. It was chaplains, however, who were least able to protect Megan.

Ultimately, Megan did lose her endorsement. Megan said of her endorser, "He was gracious in the fact that he would have allowed me to keep my endorsement had I submitted to reparative therapy. It was just something I could not do." He told Megan the church would have to revoke her credentials, and she understood. She knew the standards set by the church. When she was busy in a high paced world, she had promised herself that as soon as things slowed down at her next appointment, she would switch to a new endorsement, but she was not afforded the time. Word spread quickly, and since she was not willing to denounce her sexuality, she lost her endorsement.

Megan could have stayed on active duty. She could have found a new endorsement, which she eventually did when she went into the reserves. "The decision to leave active duty, it was mine, but, I feel like I had plenty of help finding the door." Many of the senior pastors told her they would make sure she would never serve in a pulpit again. One of her COs told her if she stayed in the service, he would make sure she and Desiree were stationed as far apart as possible. Megan realized that while she could have kept her job, she would have been very much alone. The new regulations that came out after DOMA was repealed meant that her fellow chaplains, even those who wanted to remain her friend, would not be allowed to work with her. Having planned to complete twenty years in service and retire, Megan had served for eleven years when she left after deciding that Desiree was worth more than her career.

Megan and Desiree are now married. They love sharing life together, and they have a happy home and family that includes Desiree's mother and brother, who live with them. They know what it means to be a couple of conviction. They understand that many others' convictions limit those others from agreeing with the couple's choice to be together. Megan and Desiree have made room for such disagreements with others. All they ask is to be respected as well. They now use their struggle with growing up thinking they lacked worth to minister to others and to let others know that, no matter where they are in life, they are worthy of being loved.

****

Our team was able to see first hand what civil and compassionate conversation looked like when the Thompsons and the Hodges met for the first time. They sat down together and talked vulnerably for hours, both couples explaining why they think and believe as they do. In the end, no one changed convictions, but all of them did change how they would approach the conversation in the future, and they all agreed there is room to move forward. Our hope is that more people will give such conversation a try.

As this conversation proved, being vulnerable does not mean we have to change our views, but it might mean that we can discover a much better vantage point from which to speak to the real issues with a new consideration of the real convictions, emotions, and pain of the other side

Conclusions: "I Want A Voice Too"

Anger is a hell of a thing. Sometimes it is warranted, but we cannot allow it to motivate us improperly. If our anger leads to irrational thoughts and actions in our own heart, we too are part of the problem. Instead of making enemies, maybe we need to consider rational outlets for our discontent.

My American, not yours

One slogan that confounds me is "Take back America!" What does this mean? Take it back from whom? Who has captured this "America," and what does it mean to "take it back?" I think a preliminary answer is that our country has drifted away from the vision of the Founding Fathers, and those who wish to maintain their vision see themselves as the rightful heirs to America. Though proponents of this view may not be inclined to admit it, they believe that they, not the *vox populi*, have the right to define America.

First of all, we do not all agree upon what our Founding Fathers had in mind. Second, the system our Founding Fathers established has led us to our current America. What we are today is America, the America of a framework set in place by the Founding Fathers, who allowed for change to be a norm within a particular democratic process. In other words, the democratic process is not some abstract ideal that will lead to Utopia, but a tool connected to the people of the nation and the health of the culture that influences their voice.

This means that there is not some ideal "America" in the grips of an enemy who has hidden the Founding Fathers' nation under a rock so that "we" (those who know what America is really supposed to be) have to find, rescue, and restore it. America's founders entrusted the right to decide her direction to the people and the elected officials we choose. Where we are today is where we, as a people, have chosen to go under this very process.

Those who say, "I did not choose this," may be right. Much of where we are today I did not choose either. Many of the decisions that led to our current state were made well before I existed, and, once I achieved enfranchisement, I voted against some of our current realities. While democracy gives me a voice, I alone do not get to choose. Our nation is bigger than the individuals who compose it. That is the nature of America. Those of us who are dissatisfied with the state of the nation must realize that what we dislike is the way our country was designed to work, not the "they" who have stolen America. We cannot say, "I love the democratic process," and also say, "This is not America." We can say, "I love America, but I do not like our current direction."

When we say, "This is not what I chose," we acknowledge that the majority of our fellow Americans did not agree, or, at very least, the majority of leaders we chose did not agree. We may believe that politicians change once they are elected. They are nonetheless elected by the people in the manner the founders established. We are not a perfect society, and we never have been, but we are still America.

Many of us have been raised to be patriotic, to assume and reserve a cultural and national provincialism at all costs so that when our country becomes something we no longer wish to support, we are forced to say something quite strange: "America has been overtaken. An enemy has captured it." Who would that enemy be but the majority and its elected officials? America as designed by our Founding Fathers is not subject to the rule of the majority's elected officials only when a certain demographic of "patriots" agrees with these elected officials. Rather, the rule of the elected officials is America. This place, where we live today, with all its various ideals, actions, and opinions, is America. There is no one from whom to take it back.

The future still depends on how we choose to live and

interact with one another. America is the product of us, all of us, even when "my side" does not get its way. Admitting this gives the dissatisfied person a much better vision for how he or she might help America. If we are going to change, we have to change together by having civil discussions with one another. If we are convinced that there is something more, something better for America, we cannot be satisfied to throw stones across the aisle; we have to present our thoughts civilly and thoughtfully.

Perhaps our biggest issue is not the democratic process but our unwillingness to have a healthy public that is willing to listen to each side respectfully so that we make decisions together rather than from our entrenched positions. In the *Introduction*, I mentioned the conversation in which Vernon, Portia, and I all agreed we would have never talked about race under normal circumstances. We are more likely to lob our ideas via social media, a place where we can speak of one another in ways we never would in person, but this results only in bolstering our own community, or "preaching to the choir," and angering the other so that further division is ensured. This needs to stop. We need to stop.

I admitted my hesitancy to speak for fear of where the conversation might lead. Vernon understood this, and that is why he was hesitant to talk to people whom he could make uncomfortable, but having the conversation is no longer uncomfortable to him. As he put it, "When you have bled for a cause, a conversation is easy." This makes sense, of course, but I hope we will not wait to speak up until we have been victims of violence.. We have to start these conversations, even if they make us uneasy, much sooner.

****

The system that we now have is a system upon which we all have an impact because we are all included in the larger conversation about where we go from here. How we have this conversation largely determines the outcome. Respect, compassion, and kindness engender the same, as do scorn, anger, and unkindness.

We should also recognize that if the minority sees the majority as the enemy and speaks of it as such, the majority gains another reason to ignore the voice of the minority, which becomes more polarized because we, as a whole, refuse to respect each other. We must stop pretending that other groups live in an alternative universe. If a group of people do not like what we have become, the beauty of our system is that it affords that group a chance to affect change. Regardless of what we believe, we are all part of America. The "us versus them" approach hurts everyone.

Democracy, though it seems fair on paper, will not work in some abstract manner. Large groups of people, even the American people, are capable of making big mistakes. Poor judgment is more likely when the majority and minorities harass each other in lieu of cooperation. We need to be less idealistic about our love for some imagined America and become more practical about how we are to love the America we already have if we are to construct a better America for the future.

We should act...

Almost immediately after a tragedy occurs, people find ways to exploit the world's emotional upheaval for their own messages. After the attacks on Paris, which naturally reminded us all of the lives lost on 9/11, people on both sides of the security debate began to talk about gun control right away. There was no time to mourn because there were political points to score. When I was finishing this book, I checked my Facebook newsfeed during a break and saw dozens of comments, articles, and videos about the shooting of Harambe, a seventeen year old gorilla at the Cincinnati Zoo who was killed after a child who had briefly wandered out of his parents' sight fell into the animal's enclosure.

Instantly, people began to choose sides and assign

blame. Some were infuriated with the mother for losing sight of her child, a mistake most parents have made at least once. Others were angry with the zoo officials who, according to their opinion, should have ensured the habitat was childproof, even though there had never been a similar accident before. Still others were angry that people would be upset over the gorilla's death since a child's life was at stake. Watching my news feed fill with posts, perhaps the most disturbing aspect was how quickly this event became politicized. As Megan said in an interview, "We politicize everything and humanize very little." Perhaps we should check our intentions before we weigh in. Are we really concerned about the issues at hand, or are we really leveraging the attention a tragedy draws for a political argument? Are we really heartbroken or opportunistic?

Before we attack in the wake of a tragic event, maybe we should ask ourselves, "What am I doing about these tragedies?" For example, some were angry when others superimposed an image of the French flag on their Facebook profile pictures after the recent tragedy in Paris but failed to do the same with the flags of other nations that suffered losses. Maybe a more honest reaction would have been "How do I support these other countries myself if I am really concerned?"

After Hurricane Katrina devastated New Orleans, people across the nation quickly became outraged when they decided President George W. Bush did not visit soon enough. When Nancy Reagan passed away, many across the nation felt scandalized that President Barack Obama did not attend the funeral. There are many charities that could use the financial support of the first group so that organizations can properly respond to natural disasters. Likewise, there are other organizations that would gladly receive the second group's support in memory of the late First Lady.

Of course, money cannot fix everything. At times it can even serve as a wedge to further divide us. As we discussed in the first chapter, some have greater financial means to control the public discourse than the average citizen. If we do not have such resources to combat this, what can we do?

We can mobilize. Make no mistake. When the Wall Street movement, the Tea Party movement, and the Black Lives matter movement began, the leaders in our country did take note and pondered how to respond, perhaps only to placate these movements, but when the movement does not back down, it must be taken seriously.

After the Tea Party arose as a grassroots conservative movement, Republicans began to ask themselves what they could do to garner the movement's support. After Senator Bernie Sanders caused a groundswell amongst Progressives, Hilary Clinton and other Democratic elites began to change their tactics to appeal to that group. How amazing would it be if a bipartisan movement that did not ask its leaders to shy away from the tough issues but still demanded that they respond thoughtfully with much respect and compassion for all involved began? Could we create such a movement and insist we be taken seriously if our leaders want our votes? It has happened many times before, though not as a unified, bipartisan effort. It will happen now only if we begin to talk about it.

While lobbyists, special interest groups, and major corporations have the ear of the politicians now, perhaps we can still get their attention. It might not be possible to control the reality that those with big sums of money fund many politicians, but what we can change are the results of their funding. No business or special interest group offers politicians money without the expectation of some sort of return. Why would it? That would be a bad investment.

Perhaps we can use this to our advantage. Our solution is pragmatic. Demand respect and respond to nothing else. If we do not respond to the ranting and the raving and the yield on the return proves low, then those who provide the funding will seek to put their money where it counts. Tactics will change. If they supply what we demand, let us demand respect and hold firm until we get it.

150

Right now, hate sells. We have to convince investors that we will not respond to this ploy any longer, nor will we be placated. We do not simply want to see politicians play nice. No more mere talking points. People, not abstract causes, are what we need to care about. I think deep down most politicians begin their careers wanting to seek what is best for all of us. To make it to the big leagues, however, they have to play by certain rules. They cannot control what sells, but we can.

Anger is a hell of a thing, and, at times, it has its place, but let us not use our anger as a tool to manipulate others. Let us use our discomfort and anger about situations to do something about them. Real change does not come from social media activism. It begins within our own hearts. Let us start there and allow real suffering to motivate us to do better. Let us use these events for and against ourselves so that we are always asking, "What can I do to make a difference?"

Afterword: Thoughts From the Director

My occupation has provided me the opportunity to travel to many countries around the world. I have had the privilege of working beside men and women of different cultures, religions, and ideologies. The experiences and relationships I have built over the years as a world traveler have helped me form the belief that everyone should learn how to better understand people who think or act differently than they do. Even though we are different, often times and in many ways, we still are very much alike.

One of the countries I have traveled to over the years is Indonesia, which is the largest Muslim nation in the world. The area of the country I visit is unique because it also has a significant Hindu population living and working beside the majority Muslim community. Historically, these two religious groups do not do well together. Their disagreements on religion and ideology have often led to violent attacks on entire communities from both sides. Many from these two groups would say there is a tremendous amount of distrust, animosity, and deep hatred between them.

Indonesia is a developing nation and the country as a whole does not have the same resources we have in America. The country is prone to natural disasters such as earthquakes, cyclones, and flooding. Since government resources are limited, more often than not, these small village communities of Hindus and Muslims are necessarily forced to reach out and help each other in order to survive. In doing so, they have found not only a common cause to unite behind, but they have also learned more about each other as human beings.

Having had the opportunity to spend considerable time with these people and to get to know them on a more personal level, I have been amazed to see how much they care for, respect, and even love each other. Their core beliefs and history made them enemies, but the interesting thing is that when they were forced to work together, they found out they really weren't much different from one another. They wanted to meet the needs of their families, feel safe, and have hope for a better future. They discovered the best way to do this was to work together and focus on what unites them rather than what divides them.

This book (as well the documentary) was born of the idea that Americans and those who call America home are becoming increasingly hostile and disrespectful toward one another, that if we share a difference of opinion or ideology, we draw a line in the sand, and we have to become enemies. Instead of turning to civil and respectful debate concerning the many issues facing our country and our world, we have resorted to slander, bullying and disrespect as the way to get our points across. The erosion of kindness and common courtesy is evident in politics, the workplace, and the marketplace. Before it's too late, let's find a better way.

America is a country of change. It always has been. Since its inception, America has been a country where people of many cultures, religions, and ethnicities were welcome to share their experiences and their ideas as we tried to better ourselves and the people around us. We were pioneers of a democratic society and most (but not all) had a voice in who we would become as a nation.

While healthy debates were often demanded of us, we didn't have to hate the people on the other side of the argument or disparage their character or attributes. We could have a difference of opinion and still honor the fact that we are all different people with different life experiences trying to do the best we know how.

While you may not agree with what I have to say, can you know that it is not my intent to hurt or harm you in any way? That my only purpose, as is yours, is to help be a part of a solution, not the problem? That we, like our Hindu and Muslim counterparts I mentioned earlier, are better working side-by-side than by working against each other as adversaries?

I want to welcome change through your eyes and hope you will want to do the same through mine. By doing so, I believe we can all learn a great deal about each other and work together. By focusing on what unites us, we can build a better country.

-Curt Coleman

End Notes:

[i] Mai-Due, Christine. (2015, September). Deportee Accused of Killing Kathryn Steinle to Stand Trial On Murder Charge. http://www.latimes.com/local/lanow/la-me-ln-kathryn-steinle-sf-shooting-murder-trial-20150904-story.html

[ii] Shipler, D. K. (2004). The Working Poor: Invisible in America. (pp. 97-100). New York: Knopf.

[iii] Man Allegedly Pours Boiling Water On Gay Couple. (2016, March). http://www.cbsnews.com/news/man-pours-boiling-water-on-gay-couple-in-suburban-atlanta/

[iv] Harthorne, Michael. (2013, July). Video shows men attacking religious protesters at Pridefest. http://komonews.com/news/local/video-shows-men-attacking-religious-protesters-at-pridefest

[v] Bacon, John. (2015, July). Dylann Roof indicted in deadly Charleston rampage. http://www.usatoday.com/story/news/nation/2015/07/07/dylann-roof-indicted--charleston-shootings/29815457/

[vi] Black Gangs Vented Hatred For Whites In Downtown Attacks. (2009, December). http://www.thedenverchannel.com/news/black-gangs-vented-hatred-for-whites-in-downtown-attacks

[vii] Baker, Eric. (2014, May). How To Win Every Argument. http://time.com/110643/how-to-win-every-argument/

[viii] Krznaric, R. (2014). Empathy: Why it matters, and how to get it. (pp. 36-37). New York, New York: Penguin Group.

[ix] Sarkis, Stephanie. (2011, December). Political Slander is Nothing New. https://www.psychologytoday.com/blog/here-there-and-everywhere/201112/political-slander-is-nothing-new

[x] Hauser, G. A. (1999). Vernacular voices: The rhetoric of publics and public spheres. (pp. 25,26). Columbia: University of South Carolina Press.

[xi] Krznaric, R. (2014). Empathy: Why it matters, and how to get it. (p. 38). New York, New York: Penguin Group.

[xii] Few See Quick Cure for Nation's Political Divisions. (2014, December). http://www.people-press.org/2014/12/11/few-see-quick-cure-for-nations-political-divisions/

[xiii] Moore, Amber. (2012, August). Stereotyping and Prejudice in Children Begins with Generic Language Learning. http://www.medicaldaily.com/stereotyping-and-prejudice-children-begins-generic-language-learning-241791

[xiv] Dixon, Allen. (2011, July). http://greatergood.berkeley.edu/article/item/empathy_reduces_racism/

[xv] What Happens To US-Born Kids of Deported Undocumented Migrants. (August, 2012). http://latino.foxnews.com/latino/news/2012/08/25/what-happens-to-us-born-kids-deported-undocumented-immigrants/

[xvi] Kaufman, Scott Barry. (2011, December). https://www.psychologytoday.com/blog/beautiful-minds/201112/the-will-and-ways-hope

Made in the USA
San Bernardino, CA
21 March 2017